Bruce [illegible]
JAN. 1975

OPEN SYSTEMS:
ARENAS FOR
POLITICAL ACTION

THE LOYOLA UNIVERSITY SERIES

IN

POLITICAL ANALYSIS

1968

OPEN SYSTEMS

ARENAS FOR POLITICAL ACTION

HENRY S. KARIEL

UNIVERSITY OF HAWAII

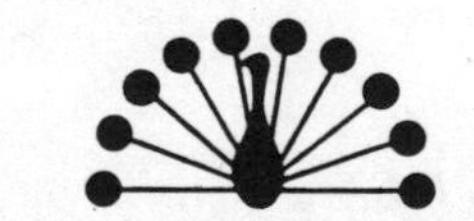

F. E. PEACOCK PUBLISHERS, INC.

ITASCA, ILLINOIS

Library of Congress
Catalogue Card Number 68-57971

2nd printing 1971

Acknowledgements

Above all, I am indebted to Loyola University—and more specifically Professor Richard S. Hartigan—for having provided me with an opportunity for pulling together what I have extracted mainly from Rousseau and Nietzsche, but also from John Dewey, George Herbert Mead, Kenneth Burke, and Hannah Arendt.

I am also grateful for permission to draw on a contribution of mine to Ralph Braibanti and Associates, *Political and Administrative Development* (Durham, N.C.: Duke University Press, 1969).

I have been fortunate in having as critics Professors Glendon Schubert, Lyman Tower Sargent, Paul F. Kress, and the members of the Board of Studies in Government of the University of California at Santa Cruz, especially Raymond L. Nichols and J. Peter Euben. Perhaps because they were within shouting distance, the most sobering criticisms came from my colleagues at the University of Hawaii —Charles B. Neff, Robert Cahill, Norman Meller, Werner

Levi, Michael Shapiro, David Tabb, and Rudolph Rummel. I am grateful to all of them even while I absolve them (since this is said to be within my power) from those errors of judgment and fact which remain to irritate the reader.

H.S.K.

Honolulu, Hawaii
August, 1968

Preface

SINCE THE END OF WORLD WAR II the political configuration of the world has radically changed. Former colonies have become nations, new balances of power have arisen, and established societies find themselves confronted with problems of internal stabilization which were never before immanent.

These new political situations have necessarily expanded the range of speculative and practical activity for political scientists, as well as other social scientists, challenging scholars with new data and requiring the testing of new hypotheses. Particularly in the field of political theory the last two decades have witnessed a renascence in synthetic speculative inquiry. Incorporating many new techniques of analysis, and drawing upon valuable perspectives provided by other disciplines, scholars in this field have addressed themselves to contemporary political issues with fresh insight. It is appropriate at this time to display some of the most important of these efforts in order to examine and assess what has been accomplished to date, while at the same time determining what new directions of inquiry should be pursued.

With this imperative as a motive, Loyola University of Chicago established in March, 1968, the Loyola Lectures in Political Analysis. It is intended that these lectures, which will continue on a regular basis, will serve as a much needed forum for those political theorists who are actively engaged in the task of philosophizing about politics. So that these stimulating and provocative presentations may be shared with as wide an audience as possible, Loyola University has decided to publish them.

Open Systems: Arenas for Political Action is the first volume, therefore, in a continuing series. Since the first of any series normally sets the standard for its successors, those persons connected with this project feel a debt to the author who not only gave unstintingly of his time and energies during the two weeks in which he resided on the Loyola campus but who also has produced here a work of truly high quality.

Professor Henry S. Kariel already possesses a well-deserved reputation as an analyst of American society and institutions. In this instance he once again offers a challenging and constructive critique which should be of interest to all students of politics.

RICHARD SHELLY HARTIGAN
Editor and Lecture Series Director

Contents

The play's the thing
Wherein I'll catch the conscience of the King.

—*Hamlet*, Act II, Scene II

CONFLICT
The ideal pastime.
Puts you *in command.*
Any number can play. . . .

—Advertisement for a war-game by the Baxter Amusement Co.

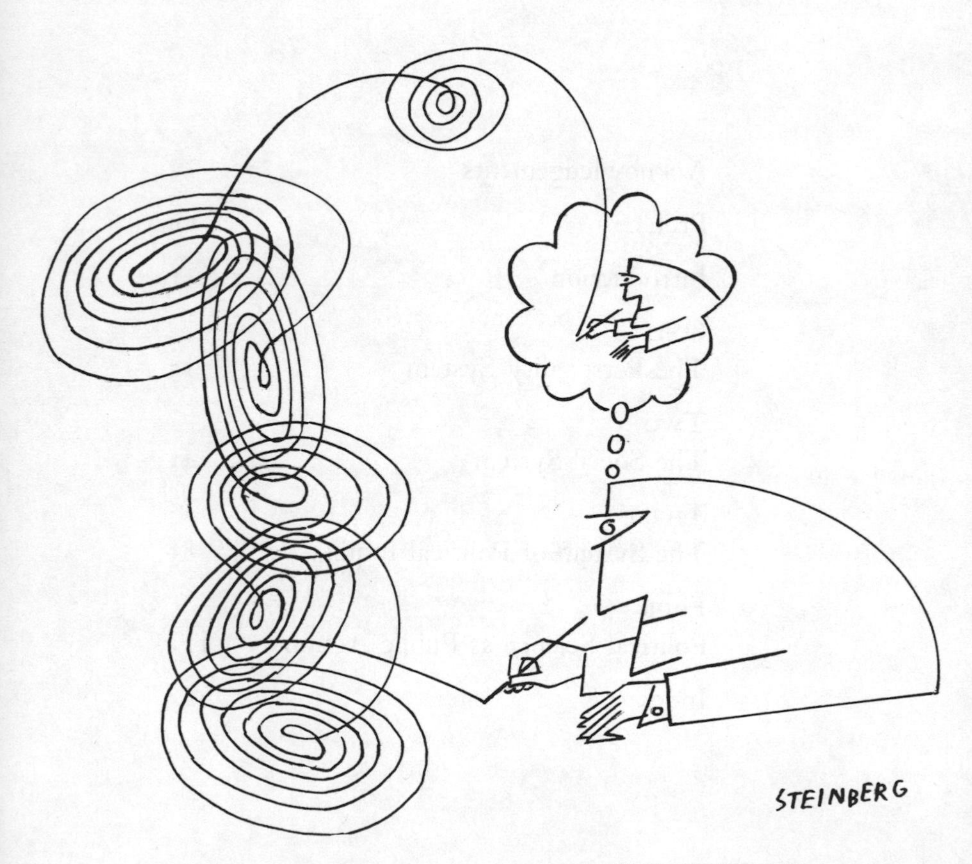

Introduction

I SHOULD LIKE TO BEGIN in the first person singular, shamelessly revealing my own concerns. Perhaps this will help others do the same. A conspicuous example of egocentricity may induce others to realize not only that it is all right to begin with one's very self—that it is possible to get away with it—but also that one can thereby be led to concerns which are anything but selfish. We may thereby learn that the route to society—our various social systems—can legitimately begin with one's own peculiar equilibrium and one's own specific troubles. We may learn that we need not be led to the great public issues of our day by authorities outside of ourselves, by men and committees presuming to certify what is wrong—poverty, racial discrimination, vocationalism in education, capital punishment, violence in the affairs between nations. Were we to cope with these problems not because they have been authoritatively defined as such but rather because we experience them as genuinely ours, we ourselves would be in control every step of the way, not only in the end when problems are solved but also in the beginning where they are defined. Just possibly, we may then also discover that a situation which is one man's problem is another's solution, that definitions do not inhere in the things defined but depend on one's concerns, and that in the just state not all concerns are alike. Acknowledging such possibilities may be the first step toward making our common life richer—more various and open.

My concern is with closure, or what in parliamentary proceedings is known as cloture. It is not hard for me to identify at least the superficial reasons for this concern: the novels and biographies I read, the films I see, the anthropological literature which engages me, the visitors I entertain—all these make me aware of styles of life which are not mine. Of course this need not trouble me. I am quite reconciled to the fact that I could not be Erik Erikson's Young Man Luther or Oscar Lewis's father of the children of Sanchez or Robert Bolt's Man for All Seasons even if I wanted to: I know I do not have the emotional, intellectual, physical, or spiritual capacities of these heroes. But I also know there are roles I *could* play. I could, for example, try to be the hero (or nonhero) of Walker Percy's *The Moviegoer*—Binx Bolling, stock broker, self-styled seeker. He is not under any extraordinary pressure, though he is made desperately uneasy by what he calls the everydayness of American life. If he does not despair in response, this is because of the specific character of despair; as Kierkegaard put it, its victims are unaware of despairing. Bolling simply goes on, dry and cool, aware of himself and his surroundings, establishing himself in a matter-of-fact way by reflecting on the world (like Ishmael), not by defying it (like Ahab).

There are a great many other equally undemanding roles I can conceive of myself playing. And yet, it is obvious to me, I fail to play them. I do not travel readily or lightly. Not for me Ishmael's voyage. I am tenured, committed, identified, defined. I still have various options—not playing Ahab, to be sure, but possibly Ishmael. Yet I fail to exercise them. I am aware not only of being limited (which no longer depresses me) but of being *needlessly* limited. I *could*, without damage to myself, test more possibilities and be at least somewhat more playful. I could play more parts, participate more. Nevertheless, here I am, voluntarily limited and enclosed. Closure, in short, is a problem for me because a larger degree of openness remains a genuine possibility.

I would strike a less autobiographical note if I did not suppose that my problem is shared by others, or, more accurately, *should* be shared by others. I assume that my speaking out as clearly as I can may lead others to perceive that they too experience a gap between manifest reality and ideal possibility. Conceivably, they might feel sufficiently disturbed by this gap to test reality by probing playfully at the boundaries, trying to discover if life might not be made to yield a greater variety of options for them.

Such playfulness is always hard to come by. Opportunities for play—and, I would add, for politics—are necessarily restricted. But to what extent are the restrictions needless? To what extent could we dispense with the restrictions imposed (1) on ourselves, (2) on our social system, and finally (3) on our way of scientifically testing reality? Might we not thrive in more playful and less supervised settings? *Must* we be so rationally governed by the men at the top of our centers of power? I would suggest that our basic empirical question, which I regard as a pre-eminently political one, is how much freedom to play, to engage in the game of politics, we can in fact tolerate.

Those in power, men free to bring politics into their lives, keep proclaiming that the burdens of freedom can only be borne by the few. Freedom to act is in fact depicted as so hard to bear that it is surprising anyone should aspire to it. To leave one's business affairs to run for political office is (we say) to make a sacrifice. Politics is said to be an unpleasant, dirty business, painful to engage in. It demands deceit and equivocation. Ideally (it is admitted) all men would share in it. But in practice (we are assured) the mass of men is simply not ready to exchange the pleasures of private life for the hardships of politics. Someday perhaps, but not yet.

And the mass of men tends to agree. After all, moving into the realm of freedom—the political arena in which men are free to play roles—entails risks. It entails the assumption of new burdens, possibly failure, certainly not some final transcendence of conflict. In politics there is no end to role playing, no peace of mind, only tension and dissonance and strain.

Thus we acquiesce. Enclosed in the private sector of our world, we direct our attention to only the fewest of goals and pursue them earnestly. We mind our own business; we are absorbed by but one group, devoted to but one cause. The alternative to such purposefulness is seen as duplicity, hypocrisy, artfulness. Men in politics who have given up their private lives are seen to be wearing masks, playing, engaging in activities that are not for us—not for us yet. Thus we continue to remain in line and on course. And when we do happen to be free to consider various courses (as students are in college), we long for a saving unity. We do not want a variety of identities; we want more than the chance merely to *play* at being a sociologist, historian, artist, or scientist. We want to *be* someone. Perceiving our various possible identities, we diagnose our condition as "critical": we say (are taught to say) that we suffer from a type of "identity crisis" for which the best therapy is "commitment." Confused by alternatives, hostile to the sheer variety of roles open to us, we are disconcerted by our freedom. The unfamiliar world beyond the accepted curriculm is characterized as illegitimate, frivolous, perverse, and expensive—all of which it is. As the boundaries have been authoritatively drawn, approved, and enforced, as convention ratifies them, we ultimately experience them as quite concretely *there*—as real, thank God. When not identified with God's design, we see them as inherent in the very nature of things. To cross the prevailing boundaries thus becomes utopian, sentimental, unrealistic. Realistically accommodating ourselves, we come to terms with ourselves where we are and as we are. We accept our situation. We do not merely play the part: we become the part. We aspire not merely to present ourselves in various guises, but really to *be* something: man *or* woman, doctor *or* patient, teacher *or* student. There is to be no wavering, no playing around.

Moreover, we come to assume that our language succeeds in fully describing us. We believe that our analogies, metaphors, and scientific theories are complete descriptions of our situation. Our words, we are convinced, do justice to us. They do not point in contradictory directions. A rose, as Gertrude Stein instructed Hemingway, is a rose; the thing is the word. Words lose their ambiguous qualities.

They are "objective," "operational," "purely descriptive," and thus "scientific."

If it should be true, however, that our existence and our way of understanding our existence are *needlessly* circumscribed—by our institutions and our language—then we fail to live as fully or understand ourselves as completely as we could. The perennial question for us is whether we might not somehow be less suicidal, live more of life, and live more of it deliberately. Because it is always possible that what I have called "closure" is more pervasive than necessary—necessary to facilitate the continuous development of our natural potentialities as men and women—we should persist in inquiring to what extent the contemporary individual must remain an unambiguous, one-dimensional being. Turning to society, we should inquire to what extent our "advanced," industrial, modernized social order must remain similarly enclosed and solidified. Finally, we should inquire to what extent political science—the one discipline which presumes to come to terms with the specifically political quality of society, namely its playfulness—must continue to accept methods serving to vindicate a prepolitical world, a world designed to keep individuals and their groups from playing roles in public. Once we have specified the extent to which our development is needlessly arrested, we may feel moved to ask how we might pry open (1) our personality system, (2) our social system, and (3) our system for gaining scientific understanding.

To overcome closure, I would argue, we must act on the premise that we are at the same time incomplete and capable of development. Action based on this premise is inevitably disruptive. It introduces conflict, first by causing us to see familiar environments from new, incongruous points of view, gaining what Kenneth Burke has called perspective by incongruity, and second by causing us to conduct novel experiments beyond the existing frontiers. Our constant self-imposed assignment must be to test the degree of tolerable disruption. It must be to incorporate new perceptions and experiences, and to maintain our balance in the process.

I would have us think of the procedures for introducing and balancing new points of view and new experiences as essentially political procedures. And I would similarly characterize as "political" the psychological and the social arena within which our interests are brought into balance. If, then, we are concerned with widening the range of our experience, with making the most of our lives, our basic concern must be with injecting politics—political procedures and political areas—into closed systems. To put this differently, our concern must be with converting nonpolitical systems into political ones.

And this is done, as I have already intimated, by appropriating those raw experiences which reduce and humiliate us insofar as we fail to make them ours. We must engage in at least symbolic action, for we know that experiences we have not succeeded in expressing for ourselves continue to victimize us. Laws which are not ours, disciplines which are not self-taught—all these dehumanize us: we know they make us the instruments of nature or of others.

It should not be difficult at this point to anticipate my strategy for counteracting the threats of dehumanization, the threats to politics posed by needless closures. We must enlarge our *private world* through the acceptance of a greater range and intensity of experiences, vicarious ones if that is all we can afford. We must enlarge our *collective existence* by establishing institutions encouraging more participation, more testing of "reality." And we must enlarge our *science of politics*, embracing a pragmatic epistemology, challenging positivistic approaches which merely reconcile us to our present fate. Our initial need, I would argue, is to conceptualize possibilities in these three spheres. It is to establish a creditable frame of mind, to frame what is not altogether present and visible.

I trust that what I have been trying to say is wholly clear. I see our present situation as a form of confinement, and I experience this confinement as a problem. I recognize, of course, that some confinements are unavoidable, indeed necessary. Total freedom is literally inconceivable: to conceive of it is to define and delimit it. Without limitations, freedom is utterly meaningless. Thus our question today remains the classical one to which there is no definitive answer: how much freedom we can afford without destroying its basis.

If this remains the relevant question, we are impelled to inquire as concretely as possible whether we are more confined today—here and now—than we need to be. We must raise questions about the constrictions implicit in our institutions on the one hand and our theories on the other. Are we needlessly confined by our schools, hospitals, and prisons, our private businesses and public governments, our assembly lines, communication networks, and suburban developments, our museums, libraries, and research centers, our very constitutional systems of government? Are we needlessly confined by our ideas, by our ideologies, metaphors, and myths?

These questions are empirical ones to which a naturalistic science of human behavior properly addresses itself. But if such a science is to be liberating and humanizing, if it is not merely to adjust us to the enclosures that are so manifestly present, then it must accommodate a conception of itself and of society offered in ambiguous, unsettling terms. It must resist offering definitive propositions, guarding against even the appearance of certitude.

One task of theory is to define the proper way of conceiving of both science and the "reality" upon which science acts. But rather than to specify the functions of theory, what I should like to do is to exemplify them, revealing what they might be in operation. This should keep me from presuming to say what theorists, if only they were wise and virtuous, would be doing and instead compel me to engage in theorizing. Thereby others may be freed to judge the uses of theory, see its relations to other forms of action, and recognize their respective limitations and promises.

If my exposition is often digressive and sometimes redundant, this is because I am less concerned with reaching a conclusion than with elucidating a point of view. My diversions are meant to divert. What I should like to say is again and again *meant* to be beside the point, a planned departure from the main chance and the rewarding order of facts, an annoying distraction, at best an insinuating deflection. Thus the better part of my argument is contained in my manner of presenting it—discursively, dialogically, and somewhat complacently. This manner, I know, is not suitable to all occasions; in fact, to the extent that matters of life and death are at stake it is an outrageous posture. Yet having found temporary shelter, I feel it is reasonable enough to speak in a leisurely fashion, adding qualifications to affirmations, multiplying meanings, injecting complications, inviting contradictions. I am aware of course that a price is being paid for my leisure: as I take time out to form my sentences, men elsewhere are being used, violated, discarded. My words are not directed to them. Nor are they directed to their wholly preoccupied rulers—specialists in violence who *know* what is just and are very busy doing justice. I can only expect to reach those in the middle who are fortunate enough to share my shelter, who are not fully involved oppressing others or fighting oppression, who can afford to read and listen, to think, and to talk back.

Since my final message is that we must learn to make our way without finalities, I realize I will in the end fail to be persuasive. But the mere fact of my persisting nonetheless —in the foreknowledge of the inconsequence of my argument—should encourage others to risk failure. We may yet learn to recognize this as the only enduring form of success.

He doesn't deal in isolated little tricks; rather, he has developed a pervasive style of relating to others that perpetually casts what he says into doubt. The put-on is an open-end *form.*

—Jacob Brackman, "The Put-On," *The New Yorker* (June 24, 1967)

ONE

The Personality System

"MAN IS BORN FREE, and everywhere he is in chains. Many a man believes himself to be the master of others, but is himself the greater slave." Restraints—Rousseau tells us at the very outset of his *Social Contract*—are universal. Is it possible for men to free themselves? Not, surely, if man's restraints are natural, the very condition of his being, constitutive of his nature. The price of freedom would then be the loss of his very nature. But Rousseau goes on to observe that restraints are imposed by convention, not by nature. By nature, man is free. He is free to be himself, to be what *he* is.

But what *is* he? Rousseau refrains from specifying, for what man is depends on his distinctive, inimitable nature, and this is so singular that it cannot be expressed in general terms. If we nevertheless persist in speaking of natural restraints, we must always refer them back to man, seeing them as man's very own. They do not find their source in some supernatural realm. While not always in evidence, they emphatically exist, woven, so to speak, into the very tissue of man. Recognizing them, man complies with them, lest he deny himself. The free man obeys—the law of his nature. Obeying his own law, man is free: he governs himself.

Rousseau impels us to note not only that we generally distinguish between two kinds of restraints, one natural to man and the other conventional—artificially imposed. He also leads us to see that our *natural* restraints should not be thought of as restraints at all, for our physical and emotional limits are not autonomous forces which act independently on us from the outside. To obey them, in Rousseau's analysis, is therefore not to submit to external forces but simply to be true to our own nature. Such obedience can in no sense diminish our stature. It is but a manifestation of our personality. It is an expression of ourselves, and when positively willed, an expression of our freedom. To obey restraints imposed by *convention*, however, is to lose a measure of freedom, freedom to be ourselves. Of course, the free man and the unfree one may be observed to behave in the same way. Seen from the outside, the behavior of both may appear to be identical. Both might appear to live their lives as if in chains; both might seem to act a small part in a tedious play on a confining stage. Yet in the case of the free man, the restraints are self-imposed. He chooses his part on the basis of his knowledge of his natural capacities. His part—his very scenario—is not fixed by an authority external to him. If he does say what convention dictates, this is because he *chooses* to do conventional things, not because he submits to an outside force. As long as his personality remains intact, that is, as long as he governs himself, he makes his own choices, testing his capabilities by attempting to take increasingly demanding parts in always more complex plays on ever larger stages. That is, he seeks to overcome closure.

I know of no more promising way of formulating the problem I am concerned with—namely, minimizing closure and maximizing freedom by bringing in politics—than Rousseau's. His approach leads to an understanding of the individual person not as one cast for some specific part in life but as one free to try various parts and thus free to become whatever it may be in his power to become. Following Rousseau's lead, we cannot presume conclusively to specify what man *is*. Practical efforts to establish an individual's nature—as master or slave, white or colored, meritorious or incompetent, even male or female[1]—tend to demean him, for they confuse some of his capabilities with all of them.

It has often been claimed that the scientific attempt to understand man reduces him, as it were, to some category, that the effect of science is necessarily to eliminate individuality and destroy life. But protestations of generations of romantics notwithstanding, empirical science has a disciplined concern with *continuous* action. It is opposed to closure in principle. If it has any vested interest, it is in the existence of an empty, baffling future, not in practical efforts to establish answers. It knows of no permanently invariable relationships. The "reductions" of science are properly tentative. Of course, what science leaves open and merely "categorical," men may actually proceed to close.

---

[1] For a case for leaving sex roles undefined, *see* Nevitt Sanford, *Self and Society: Social Change and Individual Development* (New York: Atherton Press, 1966), pp. 267-69.

Craving solutions, paid to find them, they may fail to see that the individual is necessarily imprisoned when made a mechanic, a typist, or (as in Kafka's *Trial*) a whipper.

When we presume to have certain knowledge of man's various natures because our science of human behavior has betrayed its commitment to open-ended, provisional statements, and when we proceed to inform men what they "really" amount to and treat them accordingly, we deprive them of the opportunity to develop, to think of their own unrealized future, to observe themselves as mere participants in a public performance. Our science is then not only nonempirical; it also deprives men of the pleasures of learning—that is, of mastering increasingly complex tasks.

To remain in control of themselves, men must discover for themselves how little—how much—they amount to. There can be no self-control without the self-knowledge derived from personal experience. And what knowledge of one's self makes insistently clear is that one's impulses are expressed in infinitely various ways, that the future is not fully known, and that one's personality remains in an unfinished state.

To make room for man as a developing being and to help him move beyond the conventional closures, he is best conceptualized in the terms of an open-ended system. The obstacles to such a conceptualization are familiar: habit, ideology, elites which benefit by man's arrested development, and perhaps not least our lazy way of employing forms of the verb "to be" (so that we casually say that man "is" virtuous or depraved, free or determined, selfish or altruistic, Apollonian or Dionysian, one thing or another, but in any case something quite specific). These blocks to an open-ended conception of man make it hard to find the words which might persuade us to think of ourselves as free, or at least as potentially free.[2] Attempting to characterize the free man, we are forever driven to specify what he is free *for*. Given economic scarcity and an ethic of hard work for tangible or at least audible results, it has never seemed enough for a man to be in action; he has to be active in behalf of some good cause, to be good for something. How, then, are we to define man who is free to be himself, who is, to put it bluntly, good for nothing?

For help, I should like initially to turn to the poet, novelist, and playwright, to whomever might provide in concentrated form what we generally try to grasp in the more abridged terms of science. The novelist especially has succeeded in dramatizing an image of man which I believe has become of *political* relevance today. It should attract us not because of its exotic and diverting qualities but because it identifies anew what is central to us as members of the political community.

Over the last century, the novelist has increasingly crowded the literary landscape with outsiders who are also insiders, with characters who are socially involved but transcend their involvement by being aware of it—in a word, with participant-observers. Huck Finn, anticipating legions of anthropologists, takes part in the life and morality of the shore, always interested in the curious rituals of the natives; yet his home remains the raft. Ishmael, the most durable character in *Moby Dick*, moves easily within every group

[2] Consider especially the questions raised by Christian Bay, *The Structure of Freedom* (Stanford, Calif.: Stanford University Press, 1958); Felix Oppenheim, *Dimensions of Freedom* (New York: St. Martin's Press, 1961); and Hannah Arendt, "What Is Freedom?" in *Between Past and Future* (New York: The Viking Press, 1961), Chap. 4.

of that self-contained industrial organization, the "Pequod"; yet he is not so entangled as to go down with it. Although engaged, these characters, like good social scientists, succeed in disengaging themselves readily enough. Lawrence's "man who died," crucified and resurrected, moves on by boat at last; Malamud's Levin, freighted with new academic experiences—a colleague's wife, a bundle of impossible kids—in the end travels lightly toward California in an old car. And we should remember Huck Finn's end, which is no end at all: "I reckon," he says, "I got to light out for the Territory ahead of the rest, because Aunt Sally she's going to adopt me and sivilize me, and I can't stand it. I been there before." All depart buoyed up (Ishmael literally so), though all are burdened by knowledge: Brecht's Galileo, Mann's Hans Castorp, Camus' Meursault, Silone's Pietro Spina, Hemingway's Nick Adams, and Graham Greene's Mr. Brown who, in *The Comedians*, passes the supreme test by being prepared to die for his belief—his belief in nothing more than the desirability of acting out a part in which he permitted himself to be cast, the leader of an utterly futile revolution, dying not for a cause, only for his absurd, comic, deadly role. If these characters die (or pass on to a new life), they die with ease. Their fate is in their own hands. Potential suicides, none of them despises life. All seek to make the most of their situation. Galileo is a glutton of food, wine, and ideas. He is not just reflective: he has "thinking bouts." Castorp welcomes every contact which might extend the range of his perceptions: he deliberately touches cultural polarities. Even Meursault, almost dead to the world, screams in the end that what he desires for eternity is "a life in which I can remember this life on earth." All wish somehow to experience more, and to express what they have experienced. Not satisfied with any specific encounter, forever on the move, they will not permit themselves to become fully involved by playing but one part. Thus Greene's whiskey priest is also the revolutionary, lover, criminal, savior, drunkard, hero, and coward. Silone's Spina embodies the contradictory demands of priest and rebel. And there seems no end to the ways Mann's confidence man, Felix Krull, can present himself to the world. Whatever parts they play, these characters keep their distance from them. Each of them recognizes his manifold affairs as merely human, prone to fail, none so holy as to be worth the whole of one's life.

This posture, we finally cannot help noticing, is not only that of the characters of modern fiction. It is also that of their authors. Isn't it apparent that their authors, too, have created their personalities and assumed responsibility for themselves? ("After a certain age," Camus said, "every man is responsible for his face.") Haven't we seen how Brecht, shrewdly outwitting both the Communist Party and the House Un-American Activities Committee, tenaciously put on his acts; how Camus deliberately remained the stranger first in Algeria, then in France, always, as he put it, exiled from the kingdom; how Thomas Mann used his most sober bourgeois mask to conceal the subversive thrust of his art; how Samuel Clemens disguised himself as Mark Twain? Doesn't there seem to be at least one other side to every work of art, every book, character, or author?

No doubt, scores of literary critics have compelled us to appreciate all this by now, so that we have attached the labels "ambiguity" and "irony" even to productions incapable of revealing another side. The fact is that some events themselves are, as we say, the last word. Playing the critic's game, we have often gone too far, determined to see what was not there. The life of "Tarzan" may not, after all, be high camp; it may be quite one-dimensional, as simple as it seems. Alabama's George Wallace may not be a complex, comic figure, but a single-minded zealot. Vietnam, though in many ways a well-staged rehearsal, is scarcely a play, certainly not for its victims. Some inventions do not readily lend themselves to multiple uses; napalm, electric chairs, penitentiaries, and even supersonic transports are hard to treat lightly. Some works of the imagination—Marx's *Manifesto*, Hitler's *Mein Kampf*, our own military communiqués—are so barely works of art that they are not properly grist for the student of style. Yet while we can acknowledge that some things are painfully real—violating us so unambiguously that they must be unambiguously dealt with—the literary critics recurrently do have a point. There surely is another side to a good many more things than we suspect, and we may be able to bear looking at the other side even when this will reveal how very odd it is. Thus we might not only patronize the ironic stance as "interesting" but welcome it in practice.

I realize that it is inordinately difficult for us as Americans even to perceive our capacity for role playing: we certainly do not like to catch ourselves merely at play, only lightly engaged, ready to withdraw from commitments. We tend to respect men who are true to their cause, members of but one sex, successful *in* rather than *at* something, professional in the civil service system rather than amateurish in what we revealingly call the spoils system. At the political and economic center of our national existence, our concern has been with results—getting them as cheaply and quickly as possible. Preoccupied by output defined as end-products, we eagerly consume millions of how-to-do-it manuals and gladly submit to vocational training even in universities. True, we may think of the pleasures of the game of politics, appreciating its give-and-take; but the unacknowledged fact is that the main current of our national life has not been political. Few of our settlements (our civics texts to the contrary) have accommodated the variety of interests affected. We need merely recall how summarily we have dealt with Indians and Negroes, how the Selective Service System allocates manpower, how our corporate economy regulates the labor force, or how we "administer" television viewers, patients, students, prisoners, and the poor. For us, the triumph of the groups in power has in fact entailed not the participation but the defeat of the powerless. And in our least political moments, we have not hesitated to speak of unconditional surrender and total victory. Above all, we have cherished success—and defined it unambiguously.

I note all this to help explain why it is so hard for us to acknowledge that there might be Americans in our midst who have chosen what is defined as failure—or who, knowing there is finally no way of succeeding, have persisted in communicating that in the end our enterprises must come to nothing. Caring little about the end—in fact desperately wishing to postpone it—and rejecting Final Rewards or Ultimate Purposes, they have been devoted to life as an on-going process. They have felt that the rewards lie in the act of communicating, not in some final product, in the process of learning, not in the lesson learned.

Because these remain eccentric, un-American notions, we are kept from fully appreciating even our own domestic prototypes of the open-ended personality system. I am thinking in particular of Americans whose special qualities we have yet to recognize as politically relevant: Benjamin Franklin, Mark Twain, Henry Adams, and Abraham Lincoln are fine examples. We are slowly beginning to recognize how deeply and in how many ways at least Twain and Adams were split, how full of duplicity were each of their public appearances, and how despite all they ingeniously continued to participate in their communities. Franklin, however, still troubles us: he operated so conspicuously in the political arena, out in the open where we expect men to be honest and sincere but where he was in fact all things to all men (as well as to a good many women).[3] As for Lincoln, we prefer Carl Sandburg's Honest Abe to Richard Hofstadter's opportunistic politician. (When J. D. Salinger's Buddy Glass, one of the "quiz kids" in the radio show by that title in the 1930's, questioned Lincoln's honesty because Lincoln found time to be eloquent at Gettysburg, he was promptly kicked off the program.) We feel more comfortable with a straightforward "Ike" Eisenhower or Barry Goldwater than with a devious, complex Harry Hopkins, Adlai Stevenson, Lyndon Johnson, or Robert Kennedy. For us there is something illegitimate about those who forever adjust themselves to circumstances. And what is illegitimate—not publicly acceptable—we allow ourselves to play with only in privacy, where it will not matter, where we can afford to indulge our appetite for variety and life.

In the private sector of our lives, seeking mere "enter-

---

[3] John William Ward views Franklin precisely in this light; *see* "Who Was Benjamin Franklin?" *The American Scholar*, 32 (Autumn, 1963), 541-53.

tainment," we welcome secret agents, imposters, picaresque heroes, Doppelgänger, confidence men, swindlers, rogues, criminals, and drop-outs such as Huck Finn. We who are publicly driven to *be* something, relax privately and admire ingratiating characters who can afford to be nothing, who (like James Bond) amount to nothing. Unlike us, they are free—free to ignore the calls of Honor, Duty, Destiny, and Country; they are uprooted men whose personality is marvelously split, whose loyalty is divided, whose identity is radically uncertain. We find something intoxicating about their obvious irresponsibility. And given the public burden under which we labor—the imperative to succeed—we privately envy them their endless transgressions, their illicit affairs, their calculated indifference to conventional norms. Here are lawless men—or rather men who are laws unto themselves—living in an intriguing world that is fluid and full of surprises, that is dangerous, sinister, forbidden. They are truly opportunists, doing what they must to sustain themselves (as Genêt does when others cast him in the role of thief), but doing no more. They are alert to shifts in their environment, tense from paying attention, weary from too much awareness, hoping in the end to climb the last wall and come in from the cold.

However familiar the type is to us privately, we are annoyed when we meet him in the open, for he is a distinctively *political* being, the very embodiment of structural complexity and role differentiation. Shying away from play and politics—preferring the apparent simplicities of "the country," of capital punishment, or of nuclear bombs, preferring the security of closure—we are disquieted by the open-ended personality. Nor are we reassured when he appears as Georg Simmel's stranger, Thorstein Veblen's Jew, or Karl Mannheim's and Lewis Coser's intellectual.[4] And when we encounter him in all his dimensions in the work of Nietzsche, we are privately fascinated and publicly repelled. Nietzsche's "higher man" is seen as unprincipled, cynical, unscrupulous, cruel; he offends us, implying that we are lesser men because we fail to govern our conflicting impulses, that we are untested and therefore underdeveloped members of a lower order of prepolitical beings.

Only when we meet the ideal personality—man as a political being—in the literature of social science and phenomenology can we afford to let down our guard and give him our approval. Being less aroused by academic designs, we are slow to take in all they offer—and hence find it easier to go along with them. There is little to excite us as we ponder the portrait of the Non-Authoritarian Personality, Harold Lasswell's dry inventory of the characteristics of what he has called the democratic personality, or the space defined as human by existentialist phenomenology. Yet it is precisely the dispassionate and seemingly objective nature of the prose of scientific social analysis which frees us to perceive new ramifications and redefine reality.

This does not mean that social science has finally succeeded in conceptualizing political man. A welter of vague and overlapping concepts remains. It has become fashionable to employ such abstractions as "ego integrity," "self-actualization," and "individual autonomy" to refer, if not to

[4] *See* Georg Simmel, "The Stranger," in *The Sociology of Georg Simmel* (New York: The Free Press, 1950), pp. 402-08; Thorstein Veblen, "The Intellectual Pre-eminence of Jews in Modern Europe," in *Essays in Our Changing Order* (New York: The Viking Press, 1934), pp. 219-31; Karl Mannheim, *Ideology and Utopia* (New York: Harcourt, Brace, 1936), pp. 136-46; Lewis Coser, *Men of Ideas: A Sociologist's View* (New York: The Free Press, 1965).

political man, then at least to the mature personality. The ideal has been specified in terms of capacity for innovation, creativity, openness, self-disclosure, or self-vulnerability. Yet our problem is still one of discriminating among appropriate concepts. Our terms may successfully capture our perception of ourselves as objects, but hardly as subjects, as biological specimens but hardly as self-conscious actors.

It is the need for recognizing the latter in particular, perhaps in reaction to nineteenth-century positivism, which has been stressed in the search for new formulations. Traditionally, as Anselm Strauss has noted, human development had been viewed "either as attainment, or as sets of variations on basic themes." This traditional view assumes that the observer has knowledge either of "the end against which persons are matched" or "the basic themes on which variations are composed." But the observer's belief that he has such knowledge is unwarranted; making the claim nonetheless, he fails to do justice to the phenomena. He fails to perceive "the open-ended, tentative, exploratory, hypothetical, problematical, devious, changeable, and only partly-unified character of human courses of action."[5] To take account of human action, we are now urged to perceive dimensions of the self which are eclipsed by conventional distinctions. To overcome the prevailing analytical dichotomies, ontological priorities, and conceptual boundaries, our underlying commitment, it is insisted, must be to a holistic approach, one that incorporates neglected, potentially life-enhancing aspects of personality. Whether research proceeds under the label of "general systems theory" or "field theory," man's purposes and intentions are to be

[5] Anselm L. Strauss, *Mirrors and Masks: The Search for Identity* (New York: The Free Press, 1959), p. 91.

recognized as significant parts of the phenomenological field. Man is to be encountered as a center of activity, as a living "being in the process of becoming," to use Gordon Allport's phrase.

One effort to proceed along these lines is Hans Jonas' *The Phenomenon of Life* (1966). His work seeks to break through the anthropocentricism of the existentialist's confinement to the self as well as through the biologist's confinement to physical, outward "fact." Demonstrating how the mental and the material are integrated within man, Jonas attempts to amend mechanistic, technological conceptions.[6] For him the reality to be theoretically manipulated is nothing less than the total experience intimated by a hyphenated phrase worth pondering: the-subject-experiencing-the-object. Neither subject nor object may be assumed to possess independent reality. There are no objects apart from the subjective perspective within which objects are experienced. The raw material for the psychologist as phenomenologist, in the words of one writer, is "the *intentional* unity of subject and object from which both the concept of a pure subject and of a pure object are subsequently derived by reflexive consciousness."[7] We have no consciousness as such. We are only conscious of an object; an object is significant only in relation to our consciousness.

This orientation has so far not led to much rigorous analysis, though it has been a stimulant for speculation. Thus Karl Stern has been led to focus on that component

---

[6] *See* especially Hans Jonas, "The Practical Uses of Theory," in *The Phenomenon of Life: Toward a Philosophical Biology* (New York: Harper & Row, 1966), pp. 188-210.

[7] Erazim V. Kohak, "Introduction" to Paul Ricoeur, *Freedom and Nature* (Evanston, Ill.: Northwestern University Press, 1966), p. xiii; emphasis supplied.

of man which we associate with femininity and which a scientific methodology and technology recurrently assigns to a subordinate place. Elevating femininity, Stern has noted that the basis for neurosis (indeed, of peptic ulcer) is "the flight from woman," the incapacity of women as well as of men for receiving and attending, for incorporating polarities and accepting union, an incapacity for what Stern —without making the political point explicit—calls "participation mystique."[8] Stern enables us to see how the failure to enlarge the range of participation constitutes a denial of part of man, how the drive for "success" arrests development and how its defense is an ideological reification of existing economic and social arrangements.

David Bakan has elaborated on this theme by observing that individuals who fail to reach beyond immediately manifest communities toward more embracive ones are pathologically arrested.[9] Asserting and protecting their presently experienced selves, they are achievement-oriented, preoccupied by "success" and "end-products." They deny what we think of as distinctively feminine roles. Thus Stern,

---

[8] Karl Stern, *The Flight from Woman* (New York: Farrar, Straus & Giroux, 1965). *See* also Erick H. Erickson, "Inner and Outer Space: Reflections of Womanhood," *Daedalus*, 93 (Spring, 1964), 582-606; Margaret Mead, *Male and Female* (New York: Mentor Books, 1955); and Georg Simmel, "Das Relative und das Absolute im Geschlechter-Problem," in *Philosophische Kultur* (Leipzig: Kroner, 1919). Because a feminine role aids perception, it may be an appropriate one for the social scientist. Rather than to master and outwit his data, he might comprehend it by giving in to it, risking the appearance of effeminateness. "Surrender," as Kurt H. Wolff has written, "polemicizes not only politically but sexually, too." ("Beginning: In Hegel and Today," in Wolff and Barrington Moore, Jr., [eds.], *The Critical Spirit: Essays in Honor of Herbert Marcuse* [Boston: Beacon Press, 1967], p. 104.)

[9] Just how specifically pathological this is has been suggested by David Bakan's hypothesizing the correlation between cancer and what he calls "agency" in *The Duality of Human Existence* (Chicago: Rand McNally, 1966), pp. 179-96.

Bakan, and others have sought to identify in psychological terms that element within man which Marx had characterized as alienated. They assume that man does have some "nature," though they reject a view of "nature" as a set of immutable elements. Capable of defining human dispositions which remain unrealized, they can proceed to indict institutions which function to keep man from experiencing himself as a person, that is, from becoming himself.

None of this is to assert that a sharply drawn blueprint of man and his possibilities emerges from the relevant psychological literature.[10] At best, the ideal is expressed in words pointing to contexts which deny the finality of everything distinctive and specific, which, as John R. Seeley has pointed out, implicitly repudiate conventional dichotomies:

Mind and body, rational and nonrational, I and we, individual and social, economic and politic, good and evil, defense and attach, love and hate, reality and fantasy, inner and outer, figure and ground, past and future, thought and feeling, cause and

---

[10] Gordon W. Allport, *Pattern and Growth in Personality* (New York: Holt, Rinehart, & Winston, 1961), and *Becoming* (New Haven: Yale University Press, 1955); Harold D. Lasswell, "Democratic Character," in *The Political Writings of Harold D. Lasswell* (New York: The Free Press, 1951), pp. 465-525; Sanford, *Self and Society*, Chap. 2; Abraham H. Maslow, *Towards a Psychology of Being* (Princeton: D. Van Nostrand, 1962); Carl R. Rogers, *On Becoming a Person* (Boston: Houghton Mifflin, 1961) and "Toward a Modern Approach to Values: The Valuing Process in the Mature Person," *Journal of Abnormal and Social Psychology*, 68 (February, 1964), 160-67; Milton Rokeach, *The Open and Closed Mind* (New York: Basic Books, 1960); Harry Stack Sullivan, *The Interpersonal Theory of Psychiatry* (New York: W. W. Norton, 1953); Fred I. Greenstein, "Personality and Political Socialization: The Theories of Authoritarian and Democratic Character," *Annals*, 361 (September, 1965), 81–95; Robert White, *Lives in Progress: A Study of the Natural Growth of Personality* (2nd ed.; New York: Holt, Rinehart, & Winston, 1966).

effect, existence and life, being and becoming, freedom and control, personality and culture, reason and passion, infant and adult—lose their distinctness of reference and their usefulness as counterposed and antithetical explanatory terms. . . . None of them, and no combination of them, actual or hoped for, furnishes . . . any conceptual net in which to catch the free fish of experience. . . . The clear conceptual separations and the beautiful linear logic that yielded us the equation $e = mc^2$ and the atom bomb, hybrid wheat, and milk-fed children turn out when applied to man not only to fail because they violate the essential nature of the subject but, if taken seriously, to violate as well as the essential nature of the object—man. . . .

What we have, instead of these "linear" models, at the momentary ends of long and complex chains of sensitive and never-ending inquiry, are "configurational" visions. . . . For time sequences we have compresences; for cause-and-effect relations, mutual constitution; for linear evolutions, esthetic dialectic; for mutually exclusive categories, sets that reciprocally include each other, without identity; for fixity, flux; for singularity of meaning, the caught-at "family resemblance" that belongs to words by virtue of their shared history and long but loose association. For fixity of "knowledge" in social matters we have relationism, or perspectivism. . . .

I hope I have said enough . . . to indicate that what emerges is a subject capable of indefinite and infinite appreciation; like a well-loved person *not* capable of reduction to a system or systems, to capture by categorization, to any scientific strategy, technique, or ploy, without the destruction precisely of what makes "it" interesting and love-worthy. And the method that permits that expanding, limitless appreciation is a method of understanding—analysis only in a most synthetic sense—not very different except in the orderliness of its poetry and the poesy of its order from that which the best among the dramatists and celebrators of man have always used in their effort to understand and universalize him—and them. Indeed, the understanding of the human drama not only comes out of participation in the drama, but *is* participation in the drama—and, incidentally, playwriting, casting, and personnel production all together.[11]

The deliberate and pervasive negativism of phenomenological approaches will certainly discriminate against any stringently formulated model of man. To formulate it at all is to employ terms which remain indefinite, variable, and open-ended, that is, contrary to our "scientific" expectations. Efforts to prevent anything from being finally established must contradict scientific methods which, by reducing ambiguity, keep the extraneous and the unanticipated from flooding in. Moreover, there will be opposition not only to positivism but also to the conventional use of language, to a subject-predicate bifurcation which leads to the establishment of absolutes, to a grammar which tends to support a model of man as a closed, homeostatic system possessing various definite attributes.[12]

Insofar as we follow a complacent, positivistic science which presumes to describe these attributes once and for all, we proceed to draw boundaries around settled subject areas and express what the boundaries enclose in terms of empirical correlations or functional relationships. When "man" is the object of such a science, he is bound to emerge as a strictly reactive organism. As his past is used as an index to his future, he becomes definable and predictable. What he *can* do comes to be seen as a function of what is manifestly within and behind him. If he has been thrown off balance because of some external pressure, he can recover, it is assumed, by being induced to use his already available

[11] John R. Seeley, *The Americanization of the Unconscious* (New York: International Science Press, 1967), pp. 428-29, 431.

[12] Nietzsche saw what was involved when he wrote that "we cannot get rid of God because we still believe in grammar." (*Gesammelte Werke* [Munich: Musarion, 1922-29], XVII, 73.)

resources. When his health is defined in terms of previously accumulated resources, the problem (as some political analysts also assume) is merely to provide for their reallocation.

Accepting this model of man as a closed system, we allow ourselves to be instructed about our allegedly natural limitations. We learn how much we are in fact victims of our past, how well we behave, how conditioned and personally uncreative we are, how we might be repaired when the mechanism goes wrong. We learn what we amount to, what we *are*. And because in some measure we undeniably *are* something, namely an organism reacting in predictable ways to external stimuli, the closed-ended model turns out to be potent and attractive.

A complementary model of man which reveals man as ambiguously open has hardly been able to emerge as equally attractive. As I have suggested, we remain hostile toward it because it will not be readily conceptualized. It cannot be formulated in the unambiguous, denotative terms proper for describing the functionally related elements of closed systems. It fails to settle things. It is handicapped because it cannot refer to what men *are*. It leads us to see not man's uniform variables but his infinite potentialities. Its formulations are disappointingly formal—as shown by Frank Barron's characterization of a person as healthy "when his awareness includes the broadest possible aspects of human experience, and the deepest possible comprehensions of them, while at the same time he is most simple and direct in his feelings, thoughts, and action."[13]

[13] "What Is Psychological Health?" *California Monthly*, 68 (1957), 22-25. Casting his formulation in sequential before-and-after terms, Tamotsu Shibutani similarly refers to no specific content: "Before a

Such formulations strike us as exasperatingly empty. What is more, their authors decline to fill the void by moralizing. We are not enabled to tell others what they ought to do with their lives, to what end they ought to act. Although we are still allowed to advise others to live their lives fully, we can no longer tell them which specific roles to play. Assuming that we cannot quite take man's measure and that not all roles have been discovered, we must let men decide for themselves. They must be left free (or helped to become free) to create and test their own roles, and to risk failure. Although this does not morally disarm us, it permits us to do no more than enjoin others to keep something in reserve, not to go all the way, to keep an eye out for alternatives, not to be taken in, not to put all their eggs in one basket.

These proverbial warnings, it turns out, ideally guide the

---

man can inhibit and redirect impulses that are likely to be troublesome, he must get outside of himself, imagine his plan of action as others are likely to see it, and respond to this perceptual object. He must be able to experience and identify himself as a unit. He must also construct personifications of others and impute motives and expectations to them. All this calls for the ability to manipulate symbols." (*Society and Personality: An Interactionist Approach to Social Psychology* [Englewood Cliffs, N.J.: Prentice-Hall, 1961], p. 503.) Note also the formulation of Francis Golffing and Barbara Golffing: "As we see it," they write, " 'realizing the human potential' means no less (but also no *more*) than an optimal efficiency in the transmission and reception of electrochemical signals, transactional soundness. These transmissions and receptions are *ipso facto* 'desirable,' and need not be explained, much less justified, by any criterion borrowed from ethics or theology. Any organism, whether individual or social, fulfills its function in one way only: through the exercise of its biological abilities; which is to say, through profitable exchanges." ("An Essay on Utopian Possibility," *Centennial Review*, 7 [Fall, 1963], 473.) A promising beginning for a rigorous conceptualization is Nevitt Sanford's discriminating among health, maturity, and development and his suggestion that these be treated as independently variable and not necessarily positively correlated (*op. cit.*, Chap. 2). *See* also Karl W. Deutsch's formulation of growth in *The Nerves of Government* (New York: The Free Press, 1963), 139-40.

conduct of the non-authoritarian, "democratic" person. Of course such a standard for action is of no use to the individual when his very survival is threatened and when he is forced to commit all his resources just to hang on. Unless the prerequisites for autonomous action have been met, it is self-defeating (and cruel) to urge him to determine his own future. He must first have had the opportunity to develop (1) the self-confidence which allows him to admit to having made a stultifying decision, (2) a capacity for imagining and theorizing so that he can reflect on alternatives, and (3) enough personal detachment so that he can commit himself to a multiplicity of interests and play a variety of conflicting roles. He must first be able to welcome life's contradictory claims, seeing conflict and insecurity not as something to be transcended but as inherently valuable. He must first have understood himself as an open-ended system.

I have taken this long route from novelist to social psychologist in order to uncover more than the familiar aspects of the person as an open-ended system. We ought now to discern the reason for our ambivalence toward him, seeing him as a not always attractive role player. He opposes outcomes and end-products, he endlessly postures and performs, and he finally regards nothing as precious but his act and what is required to keep it up—namely others who are no less capable of playing parts.

It should prove to be sobering to acknowledge the political relevance of these unfamiliar dimensions of the individual—what I would have us recognize as the fully developed political man. Recognizing these dimensions may of course make us feel somewhat less optimistic about the feasibility of our own further political development. They might even make some of us question its desirability. Should we really esteem the individual committed to nothing but action? Should we aim for a pure politics whose practitioners are serious about nothing else? Is it proper to identify politics with play?

Certainly there is personal resistance to taking such a view of man, and there are considerable ideological and conceptual impediments. But whatever the immediate personal reaction of those who remain persuaded that play for its own sake is sinful (or should I say "dysfunctional"?), who believe man must conform to some higher purpose, we tend on the most practical of grounds to oppose the view of human life as distinctively playful, ultimately linking the empirical argument with a religious one. Thus both Rousseau and Joseph de Maistre believed the restraints imposed by religious myth to be necessary for social cohesion. When the empirical conditions which allow men to become playful simply do not exist, we tend to argue for some sort of closure and expect a faith in supernatural sanctions to enforce it. We are quick to conclude that man may not "really" be open to becoming a creative, innovative, self-directed actor. If we nevertheless leave some room for play, we define play as merely recuperative and recreational. Play is then conceded to have its uses: it gives relief and prepares us for what "really" matters.[14] And what is really said to matter is the achievement of some result. We desire not only to travel but to arrive—or at least to have a

[14] How thoroughly this dismal view colors Freud's image of man—and how thoroughly Freud's is ours—has been shown by David Riesman, "The Themes of Work and Play in the Structure of Freud's Thought," in *Individualism Reconsidered* (New York: The Free Press, 1954), pp. 310-31.

photographic record of arrivals. We wish not only to carry our burdens—messages, lessons, bombs—but to drop them on target. Our preoccupation with solutions—understandable enough when we believe that nature makes us suffer—compels us to regard action as properly directed toward some end-product, the cure of some illness. It is then scarcely sufficient for action to be expressive and symbolic: there must be, as we say, some payoff.

What gives rise to this orientation is of course the pressure of life-destructive forces which irritate and enrage us until finally we are moved to react. Thus the hero of Antonioni's "Blow-Up" simply could not be distracted by "mod" fashion or playful sex after he found himself involved in a life-and-death situation. He seriously pursued the truth, wanting an ever larger picture of it. Only by an act of will could he in the end return to the world of make-believe, of tennis games without real balls. Our reaction to murder cannot be symbolic or playful; we attempt to master the forces of nature lest they master us. Insofar as we learn that our failure to control nature does in fact result in nature controlling and diminishing us, it is hard to ignore results. We are then scarcely inclined to play, to consider competing roles, or to entertain conflicting interests. Our interests then easily become singular: to achieve a positive objective, to find relief from an intolerable situation. Under such conditions, we find it hard to endure the strains of role-playing—strains hard to endure in any event.

In view of the case I am making, it is best to acknowledge the difficulties of remaining open to alternatives when decisive action seems called for. We do not generally expect men concerned with life and death—military officers, policemen, judges, physicians, or clergymen—to *play* at war-making, law-enforcing, life-saving, or soul-saving. Such activities, we say, are for real; not surprisingly, in our ideal world they are scrupulously separated from politics. They are purposefully and seriously pursued, not to be taken lightly. Battlefields, busy intersections, court rooms, hospitals, and churches are said not to be arenas for games. They supposedly demand disciplined, controlled behavior by those in charge, full devotion to duty, a fine impartiality toward all who enter—be they soldiers on the field of battle, drivers on city streets, defendants in court, patients in a ward, or worshippers in church. In these enclaves there would seem to be no room for politics; they are not places where we inquire about such matters as party affiliations. Those in charge of them are above politics.[15]

Thus although we may ultimately prefer an interminable policy-making process, realizing that in the final analysis nothing else can take full account of our diverse capacities, we may also realize that under some circumstances there is no choice: we then insist on the singularity of our interest, namely the need to free ourselves and establish a political stage. It is this effort to establish politics which justifies the demands by nonpolitical activists for cloture, for ending debate and putting a stop to what under the circumstance is intolerable conflict. The empirical question is simply whether in fact we do have a choice, whether we can actually afford life as play and politics as a process for the indefinite postponement of conclusions. To answer it—as-

[15] When such men somehow find themselves in politics, in situations where they are expected to play conflicting roles, they experience novel strains. Hence chaplains or physicians in the armed forces, policemen in rehabilitation centers, or judges in political parties necessarily furnish material for drama. *See,* for example, Waldo W. Burchard, "Role Conflict of Military Chaplains," *American Sociological Review*, 19 (October, 1954), 528-35.

suming our commitment is to ourselves as an open-ended system—we must perennially test our environment while at the same time seeking to protect ourselves against destructive responses.

Part of reality is of course so hostile and unyielding that it becomes self-destructive to persist in working for an open system of pure politics. Not all obstacles to our further development are in our minds; some of the facts of life are really as cold, hard, and stubborn as the cliché would have it; some endings are unavoidable. Our death is certain, however evasively we may treat it.

Yet by the same token not all the forces which speed us toward the end—even our own—are beyond our wit to master, for not all of them are natural, and not all conventional ones, as Rousseau's view of enslaved men helps clarify, are necessary. Although death is upon us in a timeless instant, we are forever in the process of dying. We die by degrees as one after another chance for growth is closed due to conventions to which we have not agreed. Some of us are stillborn not because nature demanded it but because of the structure of a man-made economy. Others remain unconceived. Variously arrested in our growth, we are enclosed because of an excess of someone else's affection or discipline. Allegedly for our own good, we are administered and institutionalized. Trained and employed only in part, we are constricted by all those checks and balances which serve to limit our access first to the wealth of the economy and then to the pleasures of acting in public.[16]

---

[16] *See* Hannah Arendt's review of the attractions of the public stage: *On Revolution* (New York: The Viking Press, 1963), pp. 123-24, 127, 258; *Between Past and Future* (New York: The Viking Press, 1961), p. 154.

Which of these restrictive devices is natural, which is conventional, and which of the conventional ones actually serves us, we can discover only in action, testing reality, forcing it to yield, whether by fighting the school system, the tax system, the manpower allocation system, or the system for the distribution of medical services. Failing to act, we submit to nature without even being aware of the fact. Failing to test possibilities, we accede to convention, or, more accurately, to those in our midst who have the power to play with us, to make and enforce convention, to close the political system and reserve the pleasures of play and politics for themselves.

To establish ourselves, we cannot avoid risking exhaustion. Yet is there a better way of ending? As we reach our end, at least it will then be because we have finally tired out, not because we have violated ourselves by denying our potentialities. We will then have collapsed because we ourselves reached the breaking point. Having strained to attain our ideal self, having thus lived, we will die fatigued, *naturally* worn out. And should our end come prematurely because we defied elites who disciplined us (usually for our ultimate and their immediate good), we will at least have done what we could. Should our revolutionary action have brought us violent death, we will at least have lived whatever life was within our power to grasp.

In music it was hopeless to think in terms of the old structure (tonality), to do things following old methods (counterpoint, harmony), to use the old materials (orchestra instruments). We started from scratch: sound, silence, time, activity. In society, no amount of doctoring up economics/politics will help. Begin again, assuming abundance, unemployment, a field situation, multiplicity, unpredictability, immediacy, the possibility of participation. . . . We know it's a melody but it's one we've not yet sung.

—John Cage, *A Year from Monday* (1967)

TWO

The Social System

TO CONCEPTUALIZE THE HUMAN COMMUNITY as an open-ended system is to make our familiar social landscape appear in an unfamiliar light. Various agreeable aspects of our public life suddenly become disagreeable and problematical. The American polity—which seems to be such an estimable success—appears as partially flawed, arrested in its development. In embarrassing ways, it fails to square with an open-ended model.

Yet while we vaguely realize this, we find it inordinately hard to think of America as having somehow failed. True, from the very beginning of the Republic, critics on the left and right have tried to instruct us, insisting on our failure to fulfill the promise of American life. Yet we scarcely recognize precisely what has gone wrong. Displaying an enormous capacity for absorbing criticism, we twist dissent into acceptable forms and then take it to heart. Dissent, as Louis Hartz has pointed out, has been part of our compulsive

Americanism: the most conservative of groups has proudly identified itself as the Daughters of the American Revolution. Thoreau, personifying opposition, is scarcely an unpopular figure. And is not Edmund Wilson one of the most respected of contemporary American intellectuals? Imperturbable in the knowledge of our success, we cheerfully welcome (or patronize) at least every previous generation's dissent.

The very existence of the United States as a political entity is testimony to our national achievement, above all our ability to create a community within which men have found it increasingly possible to demand the necessities of life, and obtain, when sufficiently violent, a decent minimum of material welfare. Although wealth is far from fairly distributed, its maldistribution has not been so iniquitous as to make the lives of the preponderant majority of Americans intolerable. The constitutional system of government has usually protected individuals if not against their overbearing neighbors then at least against tyrannical public officials. And when men organized, formed unions and corporations, and allowed power to become concentrated in the hands of organizational elites, public agencies could still be relied upon to restrain so-called private groups. To be sure, public and private government have frequently acted in collusion, manipulating individuals who failed to fit into the system. Yet not even the most powerful of private groups have been free to ignore elected administrations. Not all the policies of the New Deal, for example, were applauded by the ruling classes. Most impressive of all, the political system has been stable while we weathered a major civil war and a score of economic depressions, incorporated new territory and Americanized generations of immigrants. Nor have the problems of leadership succession created crisis situations, however nervous Americans may be during the momentary power-vacuum following a presidential assassination. In other words, whatever the costs, we *did* get West. We subdued the natives, felled the timber, dammed the rivers, built the railroads, mined the mountains, extracted the oil, mastered the landscape, and put the machine in the garden. The net output of our economic-political system—our material abundance, the exquisiteness of even our waste products—has been the envy of other nations.

We spend so much time advertising and celebrating all this—obligingly exaggerating, as I have, the success of America in granting individuals the necessities of life—that it has been hard to delineate the character of our failure. If it can be said that a nation whose output is as estimable as ours nonetheless fails us today, what could possibly satisfy? My contention, quite simply, is that we cannot regard a community as successful unless it fully accommodates political man as I have sought to define him—namely in terms of an open-ended system.

Valuing man as a self-governed agent, we are compelled to become sensitive to those of our institutions which fail to sustain him. We are led to perceive some of the most central elements of our national community as designed neither by nor for him. The man-made landscape, the passenger car, the transportation network, the federal system, the organization of the economy, the self-contained elementary school classroom, female nurses and male physicians, forty-acre farms and detached single-family dwellings—all these have been claimed to be truly natural to man, to serve his own best interest. But although we may speak of these institutions as if they were absolutes conforming to human nature, only a lack of self-knowledge can make us believe that they are more than conventional. Some are the results of our first constitutional convention, others of even more basic agreements, and a very few of the free consent of all individuals affected by them. When they fail to serve our natural needs—in particular our need to take a meaningful part within the community—they fail to promote our development. When they preempt the space we need to become open-ended persons, they keep us from developing our capacity for taking turns to play diverse, mutually incompatible roles.

If men are to be encouraged to develop by identifying one another (so that ultimately they can identify *with* one another), each individual must have opportunities to hear his own voice—that is, to assume the positions of others and overhear himself. He therefore needs others, others with the self-assurance, experience, wit, and emotional versatility to appreciate his performance. To get the most out of others, he must be able to treat them as equals however different they obviously are from him. If he is equalitarian in his conduct, this will then not be for their sake, but for his.

It follows that to establish him—to give him command over his impulses—we must foster those habits of mind which enable individuals to identify with others. Our very language must be so inconclusive and open that it can readily include whatever points others have not made, but might still insist on making. Thus our public laws and moral codes cannot properly prescribe some definitive norm of virtuous conduct or meritorious service. Risking good order, they must remain ambiguous, merely formalistic and procedural, granting individuals the freedom to improvise and act—provided, of course, we have created the space for it.

Such space is admittedly scarce in the underdeveloped sectors of society, wherever men must be disciplined merely to survive. We are familiar enough with situations that seem to justify discipline. At times, it appears, we cannot help but penalize improvisations, playfulness, or half-hearted commitments. We feel we need the fully disciplined traffic officer who is so totally devoted to his calling that he never has to bother to reflect on what is required of him. We like him to be free from the burden of having to play his role self-consciously; we train him so that he does not have to remain continuously aware of himself, of the alternative consequences of his actions, and of his responsibility to others. Untroubled by conflicting interests, he need not see himself from the perspective of others, others who might compromise his overriding commitment to law and order. He is not trained to "play" his role: he is a "natural" for it. Fully absorbed by his job, he truly *is* a cop, the very personification of the type. He is in fact well known even in societies which might tolerate less devotion to duty and more to the individual personality.

Favoring individual development, we cannot ultimately esteem a society designed for what Marcuse has aptly called one-dimensional men. We may feel the need to compromise, but in principle we must support the open heterogeneous organization over the closed homogeneous association, the multi-interest over the single-interest group, the individual person who has succeeded in integrating a variety of roles over the one who has become the final embodiment of but one role. We must recognize that a police officer, a judge, or even a professor fully devoted to his calling is apt to become more civil and less insufferable if he thought of himself as merely playing a role. Not expecting total fulfillment in their enterprises, men who presume to govern us may thus become less imperious and more equivocal. Admittedly, their signals would turn out to be ambiguous, and they would test our capacity for tolerating ambiguity. But this should serve to put prevailing conventions into jeopardy, opening cracks in the systems run by those who administer our lives and block our growth.

Those in command, I realize, prefer *un*ambiguous communication. They rightly regard indirect and equivocal action as wasteful of their resources. Yet if our laws and institutions were to allow them to accommodate more ambiguity (and to expect less compliance), would our lives not become richer? Our lives would certainly become more risky—whether in educational establishments, in governmental offices, or at traffic intersections. Having space to make unauthorized turns, we might become more venturesome—assuming we have the resources and the nerve to stand the strain.

To succeed in clearing space for man as a political being, a social system must initially do what ours has done exceedingly well: provide that measure of material welfare which frees us to reflect not only on our wants but also on our needs. On the desirability of at least this, there would seem to be a consensus, one the Johnson administration has made explicit. In public, it is no longer respectable to doubt that we have an obligation to provide the physical, biological, and psychological conditions which enable us to establish ourselves.

At the same time, however, we have not publicly raised the institutional question of how society must be structured if the nation's material output is to be distributed so as to satisfy more than the most elementary needs of the whole of its populace. Although the aggregate of services and products is staggering (allowing us to engage in military operations abroad as well as to provide subsidies which contribute to economic obesity at home), our wealth is still so allocated that its benefits flow primarily toward groups which are well organized, cohesive, and articulate. Nevertheless, we are beginning to recognize that structural changes are called for.[1] Much that strikes us as unfortunate about American public policies—policies concerning industrial production, medicine, education, housing, communication, transportation, natural resources, and recreation—is not so much accidental as it is systematically related to America's organizational structure, satisfying the implicit requirements of the major groups in America. It is becoming clear, for example, that America's involvement in Vietnam, whether a pathetic miscalculation or not, has been altogether functional to the inequalities built into virtually all the prevailing structures—the structure of government, the party system, the military system, the industrial system, the financial system, the economic manpower selection system, and the ideological system. I do not know of any potent elite—or any potent cluster of elites—to which our major domestic and foreign policies are dysfunctional. If,

[1] Consider the analysis in Theodore Lowi, "The Public Philosophy: Interest-Group Liberalism," *American Political Science Review*, 61 (March, 1967), 5-24. *See* also Peter Bachrach, "Corporate Authority and Democratic Theory," mimeographed paper prepared for delivery at the Meeting of the American Political Science Association, New York, 1966.

then, our programs and policies are indeed functional to our various structures *and still fail to satisfy the needs of the individual as a political being*, our defects are structural.

This much may be evident—and may indeed become increasingly evident insofar as our concern with the eradication of poverty, grinding labor, and physical suffering remains irreversible. But if more is required than to alleviate needless pain, the problem of gaining understanding of our condition lies deeper. So far, we have scarcely seen beyond the need simply to help the individual catch his breath and relax. And in view of the fact that even this immediate need has hardly been satisfied, we find it understandably hard to think of worthier objectives and still harder to think of the social systems within which they might be achieved.

The fact is that here and there such systems have already been established. It remains to look at one or another of them sympathetically enough to disclose its ramifications and determine how it might satisfy our needs as individuals. We are admittedly inclined to dismiss it, speaking of what goes on inside as "mere" play and regarding the players as altogether self-centered. We see it as a sanctuary and add that it is contrived and unrealistic, at best a complex, expensive escape mechanism. All of which—we may as well face it—is true.

We can best learn about its costs and benefits, I think, by speculating about the meaning and implications of some experiments in simulation. In one which is embarrassingly familiar, we arrange to have Johnny play mayor for a day. By prearrangement with the mayor's office, we select a well-accredited youngster, not to have him *become* mayor, of course, but to have him play the mayor's role for a limited period of time. To be sure, our young actor does not have all the attributes of the mayor. But as we come to realize that Johnny is far from some final incarnation of our ideal, we might wonder about the real mayor. How real are *his* attributes? Is it not true that he, too, has been selected by prearrangement, and that he, too, is expected to play the mayor's role for a limited period of time? He may be more "real," better cast for his role; he certainly appears to be more capable of controlling himself under pressure. But in principle what difference is there between the one-day and the four-year incumbent? Is either a *born* mayor? Did not both have to be worked on?

Speculating further, we might inquire if others in society might not also play the mayor's part, and if more should get the chance. The answer to this question, however, must depend on whether we like to see the mayor merely enjoy himself in politics or whether we want him to get things done for us. When we care about policy outputs, we will not let just anyone be mayor. But what if our concern were with enlarging the incumbent's range of experience? What if we cared about intrinsic rather than extrinsic rewards? What if we could afford to give all manner of men a chance to get pleasure out of disciplining themselves and mastering a new role?[2]

A more complicated experiment in simulation may make my own answers to these questions more persuasive. At the Space Center in Houston, we have been permitted to learn, a team of engineers practices giving "emergency instructions" to orbiting spacecraft. Rehearsing, the engineers re-

[2] If an empirically verified answer is wanted, we might test the hypothesis that the greater our interest in policy outcomes the more adverse we will be toward turnover in office, or that the closer we are to starvation the less we will tolerate politics as a process which yields intrinsic satisfactions.

ceive information about various emergencies, and are then expected to issue orders which will prevent some impending disaster. They sit in front of what are in effect teaching machines which raise programmed questions. If someone's answer is wrong, he must try all over again, or get demoted. If the answer is partially right, he must give amended instructions to the machine. If it is wholly right, he is free to consider the next problem. With speed, ingenuity, perseverance, and alertness, he seeks to pass all conceivable tests, keeping a nonexistent spacecraft on course and in equilibrium. His reward lies in the opportunity to participate, in the pleasure of skillfully playing a demanding game in the company of experts who appreciate one another's talents.[3]

Observing such a team play its game, we might ask what practical difference it would make if their exercise were *not* a rehearsal for the real thing. I can see no reason why the technicians at work would be less intense, alert, and controlled, for their game would be just as demanding, and

[3] According to the account provided by *Time*, the "director," Chris Kraft, runs a group of "controllers" through weeks of simulation. "They practice at least a dozen aborts, a half-dozen re-entry simulations, and another half-dozen assorted orbital situations. No one in the control room, not even Kraft, ever knows just what problem has been programmed into the computer-run simulation system. Not until they are actually faced with the artificial emergency can Kraft's men be sure whether they are dealing with an oxygen leak, an unsatisfactory orbit, or a violently ill astronaut. . . . Simulations are played through in deadly earnest. Once started, there is no stopping; if the controllers hesitate too long or make a mistake, they must work their own way out. After each simulation, Kraft gets on the intercom to conduct the 'wake.' That debriefing, says John Hodge, a deputy flight director, 'is a public confessional.' . . . Kraft prefers to think of himself as conductor of a symphony orchestra. 'The conductor,' he says, 'can't play all the instruments—he may not even be able to play any one of them. But he knows when the first violin should be playing, and he knows when the trumpets should be loud or soft, and when the drummer should be drumming. He mixes all this up and out comes the music. That's what we do here.'" ("Conductor in a Command Post," *Time*, August 27, 1965, p. 53.)

hence just as satisfying when skillfully played. We might go on to speculate what would happen if the participants themselves were unconcerned about some actual spacecraft and became instead completely interested in testing themselves in plain view of others who, like knowledgeable spectators watching ballet, appreciate disciplined behavior under pressure. Clearly, the elimination of outside reality would make it safer to participate in such games: if the participants lost, the damage would not be catastrophic "out there." The players can always go back and try their hands at simpler games. In other words, if we were to become indifferent to end-results, perhaps we could let more individuals into our game rooms—into arenas within which they could bring their experience under rational control, play parts, and be respected by others for playing them well.

To complicate matters, I should like to provide one final illustration of the character of simulation—Georg Simmel's detailed description, drawn from the sociology of sex, of what he calls the play-form of eroticism. His account helps us see how a relationship may be wholly based on indifference to consequences. Its basic form is simple enough: someone makes an offer, you refuse—but you refuse so intriguingly, so promisingly, that you continue to get offers. Simmel has characterized this as feminine flirtation. It consists of making a vague promise before staging a partial withdrawal. The woman, he says, seeks

> to attract the male but always to stop short of a decision, and to reject him but never to deprive him of all hope. The coquettish woman enormously enhances her attractiveness if she shows her consent as an almost immediate possibility but is ultimately not serious about it. Her behavior swings back and forth between

"yes" and "no" *without stopping at either*. She playfully exhibits the pure and simple form of erotic decisions and manages to embody their polar opposites in a perfectly consistent behavior: its decisive, well-understood content, that would commit her to one of the two opposites, does not even enter.

Simmel also makes clear that it really takes two to play. The male who makes the offer cannot be the mere victim of the female, dragged along by her playful vacillation between a qualified "yes" and a qualified "no." The game is complete only when the parties to it are equal. The male, too, must act without making a scene. (To make a scene is to insist on real conclusions.) He must restrain himself. Neither party may be overwhelmed by lust. Both must be in control of themselves. Both must leave behind the "*reality* of erotic desire, consent, or refusal."

True coquetry has no serious import. It is form without content. If content were to enter, the process would immediately become a full-scale *private* affair; it would then be sincere—"for real"—not properly public. But as long as serious content is lacking the process remains a public one. And *public* action, as Simmel helps make clear, is free "from all gravity of immutable contents"; gay and sportive, it has "the character of suspension of permanent realities. . . ."[4]

It may be said that something crucial is ultimately left out in all simulation. Don't we need the very external reality that is being so artfully suspended? Could one get "real" satisfaction out of games unless they do symbolize a "real" world in which decisions matter, in which life is "really" at

[4] Georg Simmel, *The Sociology of Georg Simmel*, trans. Kurt H. Wolff (New York: The Free Press, 1950), pp. 50-51; emphasis added. It would be instructive to see the play-form of eroticism applied to the sociology of education, treating the teacher as flirtatious actor.

stake and the results of decisions are irrevocable? This is of course a testable, empirical question, and I do not know the answer. But I doubt that the queen in a game of chess must refer to a "real" queen before we can feel the loss of the piece. Even games not played for profit can make us sweat. Conceivably, we must have the chance to play winner-take-all games—like Russian roulette—because they add an otherwise unrealized dimension to life (provided we win). No doubt, motorcycle racing or sky diving does take us close to nature—our own nature. And perhaps such activities are the only ultimate way of testing ourselves. But there remains another part of our nature—a part so far accommodated only by the privileged orders of society. I am referring to our political capacities, our playful self which demands that we publicly keep our private impulses in reserve, never risking the whole of our lives, not even for the possible thrill of experiencing total freedom.

What is at once the most elementary and the most obvious form of our political nature is found in the phenomenon of conversation. To help elucidate it, I should again like to rely on Simmel as someone who has revealed its distinctive character, for he not only noted that it is our most general common medium but also stressed what we easily overlook: its trivial and gratuitous content. At social gatherings, he observed, we talk only for the sake of talking. Ideally, we have no ulterior motive. Our topic is but a medium of exchange; like money, it has no intrinsic value.

All the forms in which this exchange is realized—quarrel, appeal to norms recognized by both parties, pacification by compromise and by discovery of common convictions, grateful acceptance of the new, and covering up of anything on which no understanding can be hoped for—all these forms usually are in the service of the countless contents and purposes of human life. . . . For conversation to remain satisfied with mere form it cannot allow any content to become significant in its own right. As soon as the discussion becomes objective, as soon as it makes the ascertainment of a truth its purpose (it may very well be its *content*), it ceases to be sociable and thus becomes untrue to its own nature—as much as if it degenerated into a serious quarrel. . . .

This does not imply that the content of sociable conversation is indifferent. On the contrary, it must be interesting, fascinating, even important. But it may not become the purpose of the conversation, which must never be after an objective result. . . . Talk presupposes two parties; it is two-way. In fact, among all sociological phenomena whatever, with the possible exception of looking at one another, talk is the purest and most sublimated form of two-wayness. It thus is the fulfillment of a relation that wants to be nothing but relation—in which, that is, what usually is the mere form of interaction becomes its self-sufficient content. Hence even the telling of stories, jokes, and anecdotes, though often only a pastime if not a testimonial of intellectual poverty, can show all the subtle tact that reflects the elements of sociability. It keeps the conversation away from individual intimacy and from all purely personal elements that cannot be adapted to sociable requirements. And yet, objectivity is cultivated not for the sake of any particular content of stories, etc., is not an end in itself but only a means for the liveliness, harmony, and common consciousness of the "party."[5]

One way to clarify the nature of the institutional setting which enables men to engage in politics, simulation, play, and conversation is to reflect on the largely latent forces

---

[5] *Ibid.*, pp. 51-53. For a useful anthology of other relevant material, *see* Floyd Matson and Ashley Montagu (eds.) *The Human Dialogue: Perspectives on Communication* (New York: The Free Press, 1967).

within the contemporary university.[6] If I may idealize the university, I would say that it serves to shield insiders against the demands of the real world outside. It thereby frees insiders to explore whatever they see fit to explore—lost causes as well as future possibilities. Should the scholar's or scientist's project not work out (work out in terms of result which outsiders reward), he is not penalized. The only question asked is whether his project—his very design—holds the interest of his peers.[7] To continue to engage them, he must follow the play-form of eroticism: he must depart from conventional practice and wisdom, going far enough to be interesting yet not so far as to occupy a private world of his own.

The system which supports this process can be seen in the way the university student is shielded from failure as he seeks to explore areas unfamiliar to him. He feels drawn toward courses of study that he could not safely take if he were compelled to pursue some single goal. Attracted by the unfamiliar and interested in managing it, but at least partially protected against failure, he enrolls. He commits himself to his courses but is kept from being so thoroughly engaged by any one that he becomes too exhausted (or absorbed) to cope with others. Each course allows for his full commitment. None can get it. He may, for example,

---

[6] Lewis A. Coser has provided accounts of other arenas which have allowed men to be at once concerned and detached: the French *salon*, the eighteenth-century London coffeehouse, the scientific society, the literary review, the world of publishing, the Bohemian neighborhood, and the contemporary foundation (see *Men of Ideas: A Sociologist's View* [New York: The Free Press, 1967]).

[7] For a discussion of the authority of 'scientific opinion,' *see* Michael Polanyi, "The Republic of Science: Its Political and Economic Theory," *Minerva*, 1 (Autumn, 1962), 54-73.

really become devoted to math, and not merely play at it; but the system is so ambiguously open that it induces him to spread his affections and become involved in as many projects as he can fruitfully manage. What makes academic life even more exciting (and aggravating) is that within each of his courses, the student is more exposed to a kaleidoscope of approaches for coping with facts than to the facts themselves. Ideally, his instructor makes no effort merely to survey data, cover a subject, or provide information. His intent is to enable the student himself to structure the relevant material. The student is expected to create relationships, increasing the number of his options by introducing new perspectives which make new facts relevant. In the end, it is left to the student to make sense of it all, to make his own way through a bewildering array of courses, each attracting him, none fully satisfying him. He somehow puts his courses together, weighs their respective claims on him, and achieves a balance not by elimination but by integration. The balance he creates, his program, will accordingly be his own, reflecting what he was able to take—or, better, how much he was able to get away with taking. Thus if students seem to begin as mere consumers of knowledge quietly observing professionals at work, ideally they will end by becoming creative, assuming the role of their teachers, participating in the work process—taking a part without claiming the whole.

It may finally be useful to consider the physical structure necessary for converting spectators into actors (or an apathetic populace into mature citizens). We can best see what is involved, I think, by sharing the reflections of Richard Schechner, who as editor of the *Tulane Drama Review* has offered some of his notions for what he has called multi-focus theater. What might be done, he asked, to give fluidity to theater which remains "drab, dark, static, and silent"? It is best to let him speak fully for himself:

I was standing in an intersection, and the conflicting traffic was everywhere and yet my art was going nowhere. And I thought of "radical" in its original, literal, sense: what was the "root" of theatre and how could I (at least theoretically) re-direct it? The roots of theatre are the audience and the play. Everything else—actors, directors, stage—serves these two things. If theatre was to be changed, the audience and the plays would have to be altered. But change meant more than simply getting new audiences and new plays which, after all, would be very much like the old. And since people don't change (light-footed biology is slow-moving), the task was to make people use faculties they don't now use in theatre-going; a perceptual re-education. As for plays, they had to be thought of as something other than they had been. But before that "other" could emerge in the theatre literature that was there had to be removed. The great classics no longer refreshed me; instead they were formidable obstacles. . . .

One changes the audience's perception by removing that central focus which has had their attention from the beginning. No seats, no single action, no inert building, no attempt to direct their eyes and ears. Leave the work of selection and focus to them. Shock them not by offering cruel, singular images, but by sending such a multiplicity of visual and aural messages that the basic experience-structuring is forced on them. Go beyond medieval and circus theatre. Duplicate the number and approximate the kind of messages sent on Piccadilly at rush-hour. Analyse and disintegrate sight and sound somewhat as the first cubist did to two-dimensional vision. Destroy theatre's melody line which is the story; but do it more effectively than Ionesco ever did in his "planned chaos" of *The Bald Prima Donna.* Make it all not a sentimental cry against a complex world, but a celebration of the world's complexity.

For example. Take a large, nearly square room. Examine

its architecture and plan whatever follows in relation to it. Choose a room that even when empty is visually interesting. Bring a crowd in. Begin in one corner to play a scene from *Hamlet.* The people press close to see and hear. When their attention is focused, play Beethoven's Seventh Symphony over fifteen or twenty loudspeakers; *Hamlet* becomes pantomime, though the actors are still speaking. Then, somewhere else in the room, do a scene from *The Importance of Being Earnest.* In comes the chorus from *The Oresteia,* usurping space for its chants and dances. Moving among audience and performers are several jugglers. Overhead, projected on large screens, are movies of this very scene as it occurred the night before, or the week before: a canopy which is a mirror. The sounds and sights modulate, increase in tempo, vary in intensity; spatial figurations also change—performances impinge upon each other and the spectators. The spectators impinge back. We make a classic collage—we treat the old texts as material, not as model. And we introduce into the interior of the building some approximation of the busyness that fills the outside.

This classic collage is, of course, only one example. There could be modern collages or mixtures. Performances would be unstructured or structured, but always the individual spectator would be asked to choose his own perspective, assemble his own images. Shows would be rehearsed (for there is a difference between an unstructured performance and happenstance). When we have destroyed the silly awe which a literary culture attaches to its books, we could again begin to make plays.[8]

A similar effort to provide environments designed for changing passive spectators into active participants is the work of Julio Le Parc whose "multiples" were exhibited at the Howard Wise Gallery in New York in 1967. Le Parc is a member of the Groupe de Recherche d'Art Visuel, estab-

[8] Richard Schechner, "Rape the Classics!" *Encounter,* 27 (December, 1966), pp. 109-110. Used with permission.

lished in Paris in 1960 to develop the participation of spectators in artist-created works. The Groupe's objective is to demote the artist as somehow unique—and to promote the spectator. The artist's work, as the Le Parc catalog put it, is to be "open, non-definitive." It is to remain incomplete. "The spectator, normally a passive viewer, may thus be led to a more active, more determining participation in the work." As spectators are activated, they will assume the role of the artist. To become "seekers, imaginers of elements, assemblers and animators," they will have to be confronted not by some finished product but (to use Marx's phrase out of context) by the means of production —namely, so-called multiples whose function it is to stimulate apathetic passers-by. Accordingly, the members of Groupe have sought to compel the spectator to participate by his own movements or his own manipulations; they have placed their works in labyrinths, game rooms, and streets, moving out of the galleries, providing special mirrors and glasses, anything to get people to disrupt imposed experiences and design their own.

A declaration of the Groupe de Recherche d'Art Visuel published in 1966 reveals the political implication of its projects.[9] It argues not only against the personalized work of art, the creative act of the artist, and the cult of personality, but also against the notion of private proprietorship. It advocates "the 'desanctification' of the unique work, removing its character of fetish and all pretext for speculation." It realizes that it is not sufficient simply to socialize art by mass-producing it and thereby putting it within the reach of the masses: this merely reinforces the present situa-

[9] *See* the statement reprinted in the Julio Le Parc catalog, Howard Wise Gallery, New York, March, 1967.

tion in which art remains set off from spectators, in which the only creative individual is the man definitively identified as The Artist. This very situation must be changed. A new role must be established for the spectator. What is needed, the statement proclaims, are "groups of works prompting the participation of spectators on a large scale and freeing them of the possessive obsession." To enable spectators to let go of their private selves, the new art must

take on the form of activity centers, playrooms, etc., set up and made use of according to the place and nature of the spectators. Thus, participation would become collective and temporary. The public could express its needs in a fashion other than that of personal possession and individual enjoyment.

It is not stretching the point to note that programmatically this is a plea for the socialization of the means of production. I would merely add that we have yet to identify activity centers and playrooms as distinctively political arenas.

My illustrations have been intended to contribute to a model of the social system as an intricate, complex, differentiated framework which encourages men (1) to subscribe to whatever conventions serve their needs, (2) to give disciplined expression to their conflicting impulses, and (3) to begin, playfully, to make history for themselves. I have been assuming that, at its best, a political system functions to the extent that it integrates a maximum of manageable subsystems—incorporating them without denying them their distinctive qualities. Generally, subsystems have had to pay an excessive price for integration: beyond displaying a readiness to control themselves and participate in the larger community, they have had to surrender qualities which made them different. Thus to be admitted to the dominant American system, minority groups, dissenters, and immigrants have not only had to live up to the minimum demands of civility but have also had to be competitive, possessive, materialistic, and achievement-oriented. In other words, the problem for a truly functioning political system is to accommodate subcultures with diverse styles of life. It is to achieve integration—acceptance within the system—without assimilation.

It is easy, of course, to integrate a subsystem after its components have been duly trained, that is, after they have learned to adjust to the dominant values. It is only slightly less easy to integrate a subsystem (as American Indians were integrated during the period of the New Deal) by maintaining it in segregated, picturesque enclaves administered by commissioners, romanticized by conservationists, and photographed by tourists. The difficult task, however, is one of full accommodation—opening the system to ideosyncratic cultures, to diverse ways of being. The political system will then experience increased dissensus, dissonance, conflict, and politics—all costly to bear and hard to pay for. To be sure, maintaining balance and yet accommodating relevant subsystems is less costly for some systems (such as universities) than for others (such as prisons). But only insofar as a political system welcomes all the conflict it can bear and pay for does it deserve to be regarded as functioning at its best.

This view, I would hope, might work on us as living models work on artists. It should arrest our attention and make us apprehensive. Revealing the gap between the ideal and reality, it should embarrass and activate us. So far, however, we have encountered no model sufficiently attractive to move us. We have been taught to define politics narrowly in terms of end-results. We have been instructed that it is useful to regard politics as but an instrument which, if we are patient, will eventually produce what happiness we want. Its purpose, it is said authoritatively, is to allocate scarce resources, and not to enable individuals continuously to participate in an intrinsically rewarding process. Thus instructed, we find it hard to perceive how little room we have created for politics within the prevailing social system. Where can we play mayor (or teacher or doctor or judge) even for a day? How many of us have access to our marvelous mechanical game rooms? How flirtatious can we be in practice? How extensive is the social arena for conversation? And how much fluid architecture for education do we in fact have?

To all these rhetorical questions one might of course respond by admitting that we may have pitifully little authentic politics—but all we can afford. Could we really tolerate a greater range of conflicting activities? Are we not already made excessively anxious by the disorders of the day? In view of the widespread quest for identity, would it not be self-destructive to opt for more variety? Somehow it has always seemed sufficient to state these questions, to assume them answered, and then to turn to other matters. But empirical questions are testable, and there is good reason for proceeding to test them in practice. Only by experimenting can we learn whether in one area or another we could bear more freedom without going to pieces in the process. Only testing can give us greater knowledge of society: its capacity for freedom; its requirement for consensus, law, and order; its ability to withstand conflict and tolerate dissonance. Only in action can we achieve what I believe it useful to define as social science.

The obstacles to getting such knowledge, I need scarcely note, are massive, and not the least of them are what William Blake called "mind-forged manacles." The ideology which has been essential to recruit men for industrial labor and to keep them at it is not one to make self-government and political action seem attractive. Men who have been expected to work hard and to consume energetically because this would surely enrich their private lives are not likely to be appreciative of the pleasures inherent in public work and leisure.

The ideological impediments to further development may be seen by reflecting on the beliefs we have accepted in order to travel to our present destination. We try to advance by individual effort, balance our budgets, pull ourselves together, and keep our eyes on the ball. We are convinced that you can get out of life only what you put into it, and that what you give away you no longer have. Life being a zero-sum game, affection must be rationed. There is a time and place for everything. Calculate. And when in trouble, remain attuned to reality: history offers clear lessons and the facts speak for themselves. In academic terms, everything (in the final analysis) is functional to some system whose parameters can be unambiguously specified. And in conventional terms, we take college courses for grades, accumulate grades for the record, use the record to get a job, the job for money, and money for the kind of existence which enables us to watch our children repeat our earnest quest for results. Understandably, we like to persuade ourselves that the Sunday magazine section ads for retirement plans have it right: life's golden years come at the end.[10]

If our ideological posture makes it difficult to work toward society as an open-ended system, so do existing institutional arrangements.[11] It should be sufficient for me merely to retrace the more notable features of the American political economy, for the literature depicting the prevailing closures has become commonplace. True, the view of our society as so multifaceted and pluralistic that it provides unlimited opportunities for individuals has its defenders. There has been no lack of apologists for that welter of economic, agricultural, and professional groups by virtue of which we call our society "pluralistic." From the time of Tocqueville to that of Daniel Bell, Max Lerner, and Arnold Rose, we have been assured that all is well: groups are in amiable competition with one another, all Americans belong to groups, and individual interests are thereby duly protected.

---

[10] Unfortunately, it is hard to ground these impressions about the American ideology in empirical studies. Nonetheless, I have learned from Gunnar Myrdal, *An American Dilemma* (New York: Harper & Row, 1944), Chap. 1; Robin M. Williams, Jr., *American Society: A Sociological Interpretation* (New York: Alfred A. Knopf, 1951), Chap. 11; Francis X. Sutton *et al.*, *The American Business Creed* (Cambridge, Mass.: Harvard University Press, 1956); Thomas V. DiBacco, "The Political Ideas of American Business: Recent Interpretations," *Review of Politics*, 30 (January, 1968), 51-58; Elton E. Morison (ed.), *The American Style* (New York: Harper & Row, 1958); S. M. Lipset, *The First New Nation* (New York: Basic Books, 1963); John H. Bunzel, *The American Small Businessman* (New York: Alfred A. Knopf, 1962), Chap. 3; Robert E. Lane, *Political Ideology* (New York: The Free Press, 1962); Robert E. Agger *et al.*, *The Rulers and the Ruled* (New York: John Wiley & Sons, 1964), pp. 14-32.

[11] For a view of the institutional arrangements of the market society as block to development, *see* C. B. Macpherson, "Democratic Theory: Ontology and Technology," in David Spitz (ed.), *Political Theory and Social Change* (New York: Atherton Press, 1967).

But against this comforting view more than one generation of critics has maintained that American pluralism can no longer deliver what it promises. Beginning with Herbert Croly's classic defense of Hamiltonian means to achieve Jeffersonian ends, we have been offered a vast literature concerned with the way private groups frustrate the further development of American democracy. Our acceptance of pluralism, rather than guaranteeing the representative character of public policy, has had the effect of favoring existing groups over those still struggling for recognition. The well-organized are favored over those still trying to find their voice. And governmental agencies supposedly regulating the economy readily become the handmaidens of dominant group interests. As a result, the elites of politically unrestrained power blocs—the leadership of DuPont, the National Education Association, the Teamsters, the AMA, the Farm Bureau—formulate public policy as a matter of course. While the rank and file minds its own business, the leadership is free within broad limits to determine the level and distribution of national income, to direct the allocation of resources, to decide the extent and the rate of technological, economic, medical, and educational developments. Those in command of our giant-size corporations can proceed to fix the level and the conditions of employment, the structure of wage rates, and the terms, tempo, and season of production not only for themselves but also for their smaller neighbors who obligingly use the bargaining agreements of the big ones as models. The men at the top decide which labor markets and skills to use and which to reject. And they control the quality of goods and services as well as the quantities and standards of consumption. As they engage in their diverse operations, they embrace—often with sincere tenderness—equity owners, employees, suppliers, distributors, and the mass of sovereign consumers.

These facts alone testify to the nature of the new role that has been assumed by corporate decision-makers. Top management no longer advances the common cause of a homogeneous voluntary membership but harmonizes conflicting interests. And insofar as the modern corporation controls an actual surfeit of material and financial resources, it also possesses the means to turn from profits to welfare, to make not only economic policies but political ones as well. Retaining earnings, it engages in philanthropic, aesthetic, educational, and research activities which can scarcely be recorded on financial balance sheets. Thus corporate managers have emerged as stewards of the public interest, assuming the roles of industrial statesmen. They have become increasingly free to act as if duly commissioned to form a more perfect union, to promote the general welfare, and, ultimately, to secure the blessing of liberty to ourselves and our posterity. They have felt summoned to move onto the public stage, there to define and supply the cultural and spiritual goods of their clients. Responding to their conscience, they have become free to govern.

This has been generally acceptable not only because corporate, "private" government has seemed beneficent but also because we continue to think of our society as composed of uncountable groups which we can enter and leave at will. But here, too, the facts have begun to disappoint. It has been amply shown how difficult it is to practice one's trade outside the prevailing organizational hierarchies. The unaffiliated doctor is as effectively penalized as the unaffiliated teamster. The evidence indicates, furthermore, that we do not really live up to the proverbial model of ourselves as a nation of joiners—or rather, it indicates that we scarcely belong to anything genuinely ours even when we have joined up. The PTA, the county medical association, or the NAACP are not likely to give their members those opportunities for political participation promised by the advocates of pluralism. It has been easy to demonstrate that decentralization of governmental power, far from "giving government back to the people," delivers it to nationally organized interests; "grass-roots democracy" reinforces power already centralized and consolidated under private auspices. And insofar as so-called private associations are giant-size, their oligarchical structure smothers the individual just as effectively as any tyrannical state. They are neither private nor voluntary.

Oliver Garceau writing on the AMA, Philip Selznick on the TVA, Grant McConnell on the Farm Bureau, Robert Engler on the oil industry, Samuel Huntington on the ICC, Norman Kaiser and Phillip Foss on governmental advisory groups, Michael Reagan on what he has called "the managed economy," Hans Morgenthau on "the new feudalism," Arthur Miller on the constitutional law of the "security state," Charles Reich on "the new property," David Riesman on "veto groups," Wright Mills on the theory of "balance," William Domhoff on the ruling class, John Kenneth Galbraith on "the new industrial state"—all these have appealed to the facts to jeopardize the theory of America as pervasively heterogenous and pluralistic. And in his *Critique of Pure Tolerance* (1965), Robert Paul Wolff has carefully pulled some of these accounts together and dissected the ideology of American pluralism. Calling attention to the reality behind the pluralistic façade, these works challenge the central dogma of pluralism—the notion that individual freedom is likely to be extended when the government acts as a neutral umpire among the powerful and as administrator of the powerless.

These empirical studies have focused on the myriad ways politics is delimited in the United States, on the organizational hierarchies which restrict participation to the sovereign few who are empowered to administer the rest from within governmental, military, and industrial bureaucracies —all posted "private" while public in fact. How men act and feel *within* these centers of power has been less thoroughly examined, and is certainly less open to scrutiny. Writing brilliantly but impressionistically, Mills attempted to break through, but few have followed with systematic studies. There are some novels and films, as well as somewhat churlish accounts by defectors from various corporate crystal palaces. At best, the picture of the major actors remains sketchy. Nevertheless it is possible to see that there are men at the top of our various establishments who willingly work overtime so as to play political roles. A good number of managers would seem to be literally at play, and to enjoy their game. To them, it does not appear to matter that the end-results might be pointless or frivolous. Although their deals in land, finance, or transportation—or just in options to exercise rights—may be quite unrelated to the social merits of the resulting policies, these players continue to remain engaged by their activities, only occasionally distracted by the need to show some measurable end-results, to produce enough in profits, merchandise, and services to please stockholders and consumers.

So far neither the constituencies they govern nor the policies they enact have been perceived as *political*. Politics, it is still assumed, is not a term which refers to the economic sector. Trained to regard the economy as nonpolitical, we have made few political claims on it. We hardly expect individuals to be granted the same opportunities for development in the economy which they have won within the polity. In the polity, we have learned to think of men as incommensurable and irreducible, as not properly subject to externally imposed inequalities. But in the economy—the so-called private sector—we continue to tolerate coercive organization, hierarchy, inequality, nonparticipation, and arrested personal development. The democratic life, which is universally acclaimed, has thus been safely confined. Conceiving the polity narrowly in terms which do not refer to *all* power relationships, we have tried to leave the economy to itself—or rather to those with the power to run it. Ideally, their power was to be undirected (except by the economy itself, that is, the market). Political power, however, was to be given direction, as shown by the checks on governmental action written into the Constitution. Democracy, narrowly conceived as unrelated to economic and industrial life, could therefore readily be seen as substantially achieved—even if it involved only limited popular participation.

Our double standard might have been more apparent to us if those who manned the command posts in the economy had been self-conscious conspirators, or if they had never been philanthropic and sentimental, or if a steady stream of ever improving goods and services had not been made possible by our natural wealth, or if Horatio Alger's story that we can succeed with diligence and good manners had been statistically tested, or if generations of apologists writing history books, movie scripts, and newspaper editorials had been less resourceful and corrupt. Moreover, we find it difficult to see the freedom of the economy and the restraints on the polity because the two have not in fact been neatly separated. Although the power of the polity has of course steadily grown, it has been less used to extend the sphere of democratic politics than that of economics, disproportionately enlarging the range of discretion of those who exercise power in the economy. Thus even while antitrust legislation was passed or while holding companies were checked or while steel prices were rolled back, the polity was nevertheless used by and in the service of the economy—namely to preserve industrial peace, to maintain an orderly market, to maximize productivity, and to guarantee a dependable labor supply. There is little question, for example, that the exercise of power by the ICC pleases the railroads, that the state boards of health and the AMA enjoy incestuous relations, and that the work of licensing bodies and labor relations boards are supported by the unions. The polity is in effect the ally of the economy.

This would not pose a problem for those who subscribe to democratic norms and an open-ended political system if the democratic behavior we associate with the polity had been injected into the economy. But the fact is that we have hardly supported any such democratization of economic and industrial life. Worse: it is the polity which is increasingly losing its democratic features, its very scale and complexity encouraging the replacement of politics by administration. Even at the municipal level, we know, experts make the decisions. Having become sophisticated about such things, we suspect that demands for mass participation in political decision-making—whether in industrial production, education, medicine, or recreation—merely betray an unrealistic nostalgia for the simple life. Committed to realism, we expect society to be "administered" by "public-private" associations ranging from the Communication Satellite Corporation to the Pharmaceutical Manufacturers' Association, from the Business Council to the National Association of Insurance Commissions. Legislating benevolently, they save the mass of men from the agonies of politics.

Those governing the economy play their public roles in a manner which is neither despotical nor tyrannical. As Tocqueville predicted in 1840, they exercise tutelary power. And the nonplayers, Tocqueville added, are

> constantly circling around in pursuit of the petty and banal pleasures with which they glut their souls. Each one of them, withdrawn into himself, is almost unaware of the fate of the rest. Mankind, for him, consists in his children and his personal friends. As for the rest of his fellow citizens, they are near enough, but he does not notice them. He touches them but feels nothing. He exists in and for himself, and though he still may have a family, one can at least say that he has not got a fatherland.
>
> Over this kind of men stands an immense, protective power which is alone responsible for securing their enjoyment and watching over their fate. That power is absolute, thoughtful of detail, orderly, provident, and gentle. It would resemble parental authority if, fatherlike, it tried to prepare its charges for a man's life, but on the contrary, it only tries to keep them in perpetual childhood. It likes to see the citizens enjoy themselves, provided that they think of nothing but enjoyment. It gladly works for their happiness but wants to be sole agent and judge thereof. It provides for their security, foresees and supplies their necessities, facilitates their pleasures, manages their principal concerns, directs their industry, makes rules for their testaments, and divides their inheritances. Why should it not entirely relieve them from the trouble of thinking and all the cares of living?

Thus it daily makes the exercise of free choice less useful and rarer, restricts the activity of free will within a narrower compass, and little by little robs each citizen of the proper use of his own faculties.[12]

It is hard to stop quoting Tocqueville and easy to use him to overstate the argument. The fact is that the division between the actors within our establishments and the nonactors outside is not as sharp as he implied. Reality is more blurred than social typology allows. The outside shades into the inside, and boundaries are not clearly drawn. Yet abstract types of the kind Tocqueville delineated can serve analytical purposes. Dramatizing extremes, they reveal the less extreme behavior patterns in the grey area between the poles of our existence. Because Tocqueville's typology exaggerates (was indeed designed to exaggerate), it should serve to alert us to relevant but still concealed parts of contemporary reality.

Obligated to provide for more than our material welfare, hoping for something more than a nation of industrious and satiated men, we cannot be satisfied with a mere increase in the production of goods. It is hard to say this. In the face of avoidable misery and pain, it seems callous to disregard the benefits of economic growth. We understandably want increased productivity, and want existing products to be tastier, quieter, less perishable. Yet while fully supporting the case for satisfying these needs, perhaps we can detach

---

[12] Alexis de Tocqueville, *Democracy in America*, trans. George Lawrence (New York: Harper & Row, 1966), pp. 666-67. Tocqueville went on to speculate (p. 708) about the possible consequences of the ascendancy of the military and concluded that this would make little difference: "I am convinced that in such a case there would be a sort of fusion between the ways of clerks and soldiers. The administration would adopt something of the spirit of an army, and the army would take over some of the ways of civil administration."

ourselves from present urgencies and raise our sights. Is it not true that it remains preeminently essential to enlarge the political arena, to open our organizational hierarchies and introduce society to those rewards of politics which elites have succeeded in keeping for themselves?

To move in this direction requires acknowledging that democracy demands something more than satisfying our conventional political demands. Conventionally, we regard it as sufficient for the interested part of the electorate to have the opportunity to exercise periodic control over the leadership of society. The definition of democracy which has become authoritative is that of Joseph Schumpeter, who said that "democracy means only that the people have the opportunity of accepting or refusing the men who are to rule them."[13]

Against this modest view, I have been stressing that something more is essential, that indeed we should ultimately accept as democratic nothing less than a society all of whose members are active participants in an interminable process—*and who will not mind such activity*. Anything less ought to arouse us, leading us to assail whatever conventions compel us to compromise. Thus whatever may seem good enough for the moment, there would seem to be no reason to *settle* for a polity which balances an inequalitarian process for arriving at decisions with an equalitarian one for remaining indecisive.[14] Acknowledging that the first half of this formula may be necessary—imposed on us by

[13] Joseph Schumpeter, *Capitalism, Socialism, and Democracy* (New York: Harper & Row, 1950), p. 285; also *see* p. 269.

[14] The balanced position is held by Peter Bachrach, *The Theory of Democratic Elitism: A Critique* (Boston: Little, Brown, 1966). While stressing that democracy should be defined as a process allowing for participation, he nevertheless insists on "realistically" making room for the elitist view that democracy is a method for getting end-results (pp. 6-7).

forces we remain powerless to master—we may yet persist in working toward the equalitarian ideal.

Of course there is an understandable fear of equality, a concern about the consequences of extending the reach of what we regard as the devices of politics. Recent totalitarian movements have taught us to beware. As the fate of the Weimar Republic makes clear, "politics" has repeatedly invaded and corrupted cultural enclaves within which men had been creatively at play. So-called political rulers have used the machinery of culture to satisfy messianic drives, fulfill inhuman norms, and build the most hideous of monuments. Culture, we know too well, has been forcefully subordinated to goal-oriented systems; it has been compelled to conform and deliver. Yet recognizing authentic politics as altogether indifferent to end-results, can we not welcome its extension and push toward equality, thereby activating individuals who are citizens in name only? True, systems ruled by goal-oriented men have effectively eradicated cultural activities, usually in behalf of future generations which would not have to be driven so hard. The acceptance of discipline and the surrender of culture have been the advertised price we must pay for progress. But in the absence of proof that the price must be paid, do we have to accept the case against the expansion of politics? Does it not have to be shown that we cannot afford the kind of agonizing play which is politics at its most authentic?

To determine whether it is actually true that we are victims of ungovernable forces, we have no alternative but to engage in experimental probing. Such probing requires that we try whenever and wherever possible to inject politics into closed systems. As Nevitt Sanford has argued, "To induce a desirable change—toward further growth or development or toward greater health—we have to think in terms of what would upset the existing equilibrium, produce instability, set in motion activity leading to stabilization on a higher level."[15]

Yet even as we muster the will to move ahead, we are distracted by our ideology of laissez-faire, our nineteenth-century liberal faith in the self-activated individual. Our problem, therefore, is to remain loyal to the ideal of man as autonomous actor while creating the conditions which induce him to risk losing his balance, which make him conscious of his own need to grow.

He will certainly not experience this need under all conditions. When he has been defeated by false expectations or by others, he will be listless and apathetic. The problem is to arouse him, to provide the social settings which allow him to discover and name his various desires. Moreover, he must be enabled to weigh and balance his desires without feeling overwhelmed by the task. In other words, he must be awakened to the diverse impulses stirring within him and learn about his capacity for identifying and managing them.

It is not hard to find experimental support for these propositions. From the vast amount of work which has been done on stimulation and experience in infancy, O. J. Harvey has concluded that the central prerequisite for developing the capacity to "differentiate and integrate" is exposure to diversity. A progressively wider range of objects compels the individual to integrate his experiences on an ever more abstract level:

---

[15] *Op. cit.*, p. 37.

To be maximally effective for producing articulated and integrated cognitive systems the input must always be *optimally discrepant from the intra-subject baseline in relation to which they are gauged and assigned their psychological weight.* If the discrepancy is too small or *suboptimal*, boredom may result, and if this should become persistent the subject may adapt to the situation of too little stimulation and subsequently react to novelty or deviant events with aversion. If the baseline event discrepancy is too great or *superoptimal* for the particular subject at the particular time of stimulation, avoidance of novelty and tendencies toward constriction of the baseline on subsequent occasions might also result. If, on the other hand, the situation presented to the subject is optimally discrepant it will be experienced as a positive challenge, will give rise to exploration and will contribute toward the system being articulated and expanded to include the previously deviant input.

Of course, what is optimal stimulation or discrepancy for one subject might well be too much for a second and too little for a third. The idiosyncratic baseline to which the input must be anchored is not only a function of the breadth and depth of diverse exposures, but also is affected by native abilities of the organism and by the action of the training agent in connection with the exposures.[16]

In similar terms, Leonard C. Feldstein has noted that individuals actualize their potentialities in environments

[16] O. J. Harvey, "System Structure, Flexibility and Creativity," in O. J. Harvey (ed.), *Experience, Structure and Adaptability* (New York: Springer, 1966), pp. 63-4; emphasis in the original. The following other studies by Harvey also deal with the determinants of personal autonomy, role playing, creativity, and innovative capacity: "Cognitive Determinant of Role Playing," Technical Report No. 3, Contract Nonr. 1147(07), University of Colorado, 1963; "Some Situational and Cognitive Determinants of Dissonance Resolution," *Journal of Personality and Social Psychology*, 1 (April, 1965), 349-55; and "Some Cognitive and Affective Determinants of Differentiation and Integration," Technical Report No. 8, Contract Nonr. 1147(07), University of Colorado, 1963 (with R. S. Wyer and J. E. Hautaluoma). *See* also Max Bruck, "A Review of Social and Psychological Factors Associated with Creativity and Innovation," in Charles Press and Alan Arian (eds.), *Empathy and Ideology* (Chicago: Rand McNally, 1966), Chap. 2.

which impel them to respond with "configurations of beliefs, judgments, motives, attitudes." Should the configuration be too inert,

> one responds stereotypically to new experience, alienated from some of his human powers. But should it be too fluid, one becomes amorphous and incapable of consistent and decisive action. The "I" . . . is only fully experienced when the proper balance between fluidity and fixity is maintained.[17]

Development is promoted by settings sufficiently open and challenging to encourage the individual to become equivocal and multi-dimensional—to become a *person*. They must accommodate not only the self as acquisitive and achievement-oriented but also as generous and process-oriented. The problem today, given our commitment to the satisfaction of human needs, is institutionally to satisfy man's expressive, communal self, to support associations which, by offering intrinsic rewards, serve to mitigate the effects of the merely acquisitive self and the merely instrumental organization.[18] More radically, however, I would insist that strengthening communal as opposed to individualistic tendencies requires support of characteristically feminine roles. It requires an environment sufficiently diversified and pluralistic to make the playing of oddly new roles a genuinely inviting option.[19]

---

[17] Leonard C. Feldstein, "Toward a Concept of Integrity," *Annals of Psychotherapy*, 1 (1961), p. 84.

[18] For an application to organizations of the intrinsic-extrinsic distinction, *see* Daniel Katz and Robert L. Kahn, *The Social Psychology of Organizations* (New York: John Wiley & Sons, 1966), pp. 117-19.

[19] This plea reverses the conventional definition of an *underdeveloped* system as one whose members are generalists engaged in a great diversity of activities and a *developed* system as one whose members are specialists. Conventionally, it is noted that "actors in the political process in Western societies are likely to have more clearly defined and more specific roles than those in non-Western societies. In the latter

Man's repressed capacities tend to develop when we provide opportunities for new encounters and keep such encounters from being overwhelming and paralyzing. Since the institutions which maximize the range of manageable experience are best regarded as political, and since our aim is to promote man as a political being, it follows that we must seek to inject politics—political procedures and political arenas—into currently closed administrative systems or, to put this differently, with converting administrative systems into political ones.

What might be the proper role for an action-oriented social science in fostering such a conversion, that is, in promoting the *political* development of society? There are clues to an answer in Bruno Bettelheim's report on his successes with autistic children at the University of Chicago's Orthogenic School. His very approach, I think, suggests the basis for dealing with a society in disarray, one which resembles Bettelheim's individual cases. Infantile autism, as he describes it in *The Empty Fortress* (1967), is the condition of children who are wholly bewildered, given to either total withdrawal or mindless violence. They fail altogether to relate. They remain locked in and will not say "I." To see and define themselves—and then to establish connections with others—they must unlearn what they have been trained to accept: the disciplines which have

. . . there is generally a high degree of substitutability of roles. . . ." The authors of such statements, one may assume, classify Western societies as more developed. Presumably, they regard it as proper for individuals to be specialists in fixed positions within structurally differentiated political systems. The arrested development of individuals is acknowledged to be the price that must be paid for a viable regime, i.e., the United States. (The quotation is from George Mct. Kahin, Guy J. Pauker, and Lucian W. Pye, "Comparative Politics of Non-Western Countries," *American Political Science Review,* 49 [December, 1955], p. 1026.)

killed their natural inclination to play and to express themselves, to symbolize and to talk. They must first be helped to go back in time and then to integrate personally what had been impersonally imposed.

Bettelheim's work clarifies the demands on the psychologist involved in personality building. To succeed as therapist and educator, he must encourage children to act out by accepting their every outburst, by responding affirmatively to their most attenuated efforts to communicate, their most private languages. At the same time, he must resist every temptation to impose order on children from the outside, rejecting all efforts to recondition them by the ultimately self-destructive technique of reinforcing approved behavior.

If Bettelheim's young patients are but extreme cases—if *all* of us remain partially autistic—his approach to healing would seem to have general relevance for the body politic. However developed a society may deem itself to be, it too is always at least partially autistic—that is, arrested in its development, not wholly capable of integrating new experiences, not fully articulate, suffering from shocks and depressions aggravated by a system of checks and balances which retards actions. The social scientist who presumes to be as devoted to further social development as the psychologist is to freeing autistic children would have to be no less the participant-observer. He would have to be infinitely open and patient, receptive to unspoken intimations and barely expressed needs. He would have to accept unseemly gestures and dirty words, grateful for each of them, encouraging society to come to terms with infantile forms of behavior, with extremism and violence. By making society's unsymbolized experiences public and vivid (whether in books, films, lecture halls, schools, or theaters), he would be helping it to integrate impulses he has participated in naming. Like the psychologist, he would have to provide specific occasions which impel violated and neglected groups to identify themselves. He would have to design environments which encourage otherwise unrepresented groups to present themselves in public. Thus he would speak *for* them until they would finally become inspired to act for themselves. To be sure, he may not have the emotional, intellectual, and financial resources to move in this direction. But in that case he could still proceed to expose and repudiate programs which compel unestablished groups to embrace presently established styles of life.

It is of course easy to prescribe this. Although we know what kind of policies enable men to become political beings,[20] we have scarcely perceived how much piety and virtue blocks the way. To break out and test reality, we must still confront the historical situation Hannah Arendt defined after the Second World War. Reacting to twentieth-century totalitarianism, she attempted to face the collapse of conventional foundations and, like Nietzsche, to affirm what could no longer be denied:

Whether we like it or not, we have long ceased to live in a world in which the faith in the Judeo-Christian myth of crea-

[20] Perhaps the best educational model is the psychoanalytic setting which impels both patient and doctor to become increasingly aware of themselves. As Freud saw psychoanalysis, it seeks therapeutically "to strengthen the ego, to make it more independent of the superego, to widen its field of perception and enlarge its organization, so that it can appropriate fresh portions of the id." (Sigmund Freud, "New Introductory Lectures," in *Complete Psychological Works* [London: Hogarth Press, 1964], XXII, 80.) Although Plato, Rousseau, and Dewey make odd companions, they too delineated the relevant model; see especially R. C. Lodge, *Plato's Theory of Education* (New York: Harcourt, Brace, 1947).

tion is secure enough to constitute a basis and source of authority for actual laws, and we certainly believe . . . in a universal cosmos of which man was a part and whose natural laws he had to imitate and conform to. . . .

Our new difficulty is that we start from a fundamental distrust of everything merely *given*, a distrust of all laws and prescriptions, moral or social, that are deduced from a given, comprehensive universal whole. This difficulty involves the sources of authority of law and questions the ultimate goals of political organizations and communities; it forces us not only to find and devise new laws, but to find and devise their very measure, the yardstick of good and evil, the principle of their source. For man, in the sense of the nature of man, is no longer the measure, despite what the new humanists would have us believe. Politically, this means that before drawing up the constitution of a new body politic, we shall have to create—not merely discover—a new foundation for human community as such.

In historical terms this would mean not the end of history, but its first consciously planned beginning. . . .[21]

To proceed to make history (which is what may be meant by reality-testing), we must be willing to see both our individual selves and our society as at least partially self-made. We must act like those who drafted the United States Constitution, men who quite deliberately went to work to design the future, to make history. Self-possessed, they regarded political institutions as mechanisms one could rationally construct to satisfy one's various needs. If their conception of human needs was narrower than ours (perhaps because they were less justified in trusting men to be generous toward one another), we can nonetheless share their underlying intent. Like them, we too can aim at

[21] Hannah Arendt, *The Origins of Totalitarianism* (New York: Harcourt, Brace, 1951), pp. 434-36.

providing for a maximum of self-government, while being grateful for having more material resources, for being more in possession of ourselves and the world we inhabit. Like them, we can aim at removing needless hindrances to individual and social development—including those which exist only in our minds.

One hindrance is our failure to see that the contemporary world has been emptied of what used to be known quite simply as values. This does not mean values remain inoperative: men continue to be killed for the sake of Truth, Justice, Virtue, or Honor. It means only that these values can no longer be sustained; that, without lying, we can no longer ask anyone to sacrifice his future for any one of them. Witnessing the extinction of these great finalities, some of us have become anxious and frantic. We wish somehow to cling to values, to recover them at least on special days. We tend to see the value-free world as but a desert, and claim that we are near despair.

Our need today, I think, is not to deny the emptiness ahead but to affirm and sanctify it, recognizing it as our opportunity for collective action. Once sufficiently mature not only to confront but also to exult in an open world, we may be more able to reject conditions which compel us to lie. We may then proceed to build social environments that enable us to embrace others without smothering them. Such environments would provide us with temporary shelters. Finding protection, more of us may be able to move ahead—doing so despite our knowledge that in the end we must be deprived of victory because we cannot fully communicate our discovery to others.

Men did not begin to shoot because there were ready-made targets to aim at. They made things into targets by shooting at them, and then made special targets to make shooting more significantly interesting.

—John Dewey, *Human Nature and Conduct* (1922)

THREE

The System of Political Inquiry

WE FOREVER LIMIT OUR HORIZON, Nietzsche observed, for the sake of life. To live, to move ahead, we cling to established myths, rituals, metaphors, theories, and ideologies. Ignoring unsightly or embarrassing alternatives, we are able to go on. We need lies, deceptions, falsehoods, finalities. We need to reduce one set of phenomena to another, draw boundaries, accept parameters. How else keep track of the flow of experience? How else learn one's place and communicate? Without repression, how could we bear up and speak out? Would it not be lethal—destructive of our conscious selves—if we were to keep extending the range of experience indefinitely, crashing through every boundary until, at last, we find ourselves absorbed and annihilated by an unstructured, boundless continuum, entering Nietzsche's Dionysian world without beginning or end?

I raise these questions because keeping them in mind

should make us cautious as we assail the contemporary closures in the social sciences. These questions should remind us of the services social science has performed. While urging openness, we should always recall the great good social science has done so far. However unwittingly, it has been performing acts of mercy. It has helped man repress hundreds of dirty little secrets (in D. H. Lawrence's phrase), and many big ones. It has made life easier—at least for some of us. And who would blame its practitioners? "When a slave in prison dreams that he is free and relieved of his chains," Nietzsche asked, "who would be callous as to waken him and tell him that he is merely dreaming?"

There is little to indicate that the sciences concerned with contemporary public life have disturbed our dreams. On the contrary, they have helped make our lives cleaner and more bearable. Just as a dream of an iceberg floating by keeps us asleep when our blanket has slipped off the bed, the report of political science that apathy is a function of a healthy political system reconciles us to the exploitation of part of the body politic. Political scientists consolingly reveal that whatever happens is *really* no accident. They disclose the existence of underlying patterns—patterns assumed to lie in nature, imposed by Fate, History, Rationality, or the Logic of Events. Relying on Einstein's metaphysical sentiments, they assume that God does not play dice. Like the great works of theology and art, their rationalizations fill a human need: they make our existence tolerable. And like the great achievements of technology, they help implement what the powerful allege to be the consensus; they show us how to administer society so that men cheerfully build pyramids and irrigation systems, fight disease and one another, manage offices, airline terminals, and prison compounds.

To be sure, so far the number of political scientists on call for such service has been quite limited. But the present generation, as Gabriel Almond has pointed out, would seem to be larger than all previous ones together.[1] Moreover, in the past, political inquiry was more concerned with elucidating the competing purposes of social life than with developing a technology to realize them. Only when confronted by a situation as obviously evil as tyranny, civil war, or genocide did political writers inquire how to *do* good, hoping (like Hobbes) that their analysis would fall into the hands of a sovereign with the power to act, believing (like Tocqueville) that an enlightened elite would forestall disaster, or working (like Marx) to impose their will on history. When not facing unambiguous catastrophe, they tended to assume a relaxed, ambiguous posture, pleased by the diversity of possible purposes, not insisting on pattern and regularity. Perhaps reluctant to know or communicate too much, they wrote obscurely; generous with words, they acted like members of the gentry ignorant of the price the many pay for the leisure of the few.

---

[1] "Up to the time of the founding of the American Political Science Association, and going all the way back more than two millennia to Plato, the total number of political philosophers and theorists who had contributed to systematic speculation about and study of politics did not exceed a few hundred. In 1903 the fledging American Political Science Association numbered a little over 200 members. In 1934 there were 1,800 members of the Association; in 1944, 3,200; in 1954, 6,000; and in 1966, 15,000. The expectation is that membership will exceed 20,000 in the 1970's." ("Political Theory and Political Science," *American Political Science Review*, 60 [December, 1966], 869). It remains of course arguable whether the kind of contribution made by the new legions of political scientists is significantly comparable to that of the original "few hundred."

The newer social scientists, on the contrary, are certainly more moved to construct a science of means so as to achieve obviously humane, liberal-democratic ends. When children labor in coal mines or when international conflict defies all rationality it would seem time to be done with philosophizing. Turning away from the task of delineating what men need (don't we *know?*), they record what men in the aggregate demand. They chart the behavior of voters and nonvoters, pressure groups and congressional committees, civic leaders and Supreme Court justices, weapons systems and underdeveloped nations. They are preoccupied by the flow and counterflow of power, whatever its source. They have thus turned from ideals to attitudes, from great men to the mass of men, from action to behavior, from singular events to patterns and regularities, from politics to what Christian Bay has called pseudo-politics.

In this democratization of scholarship, they may of course be betraying a class bias. The rise of behavioralists as stewards of the social sciences can in part be understood, I believe, as a function of the ascendancy of an academic proletariat. The new scientists disdain a tradition of scholarship which produced essays, commentaries, *belles lettres*, dialogues, or merely "history." In place of leisurely and inconclusive discussions, their concern (at least in the present phase of their development) has been with results. Breaking up an older academic establishment they have been vigorously reorganizing and specializing. Their specialization may be seen as a triumph over gentility, over the complacent insistence by patrician statesmen and the academicians who have served them that a general humanistic education is enough and that the language for discourse is best learned by those who have family connections, who have "background" rather than skills which might be more easily measured.

The new science may be seen to flourish in an egalitarian society which treats problems as amenable to technical solutions and which requires diligent technicians to serve it. Perhaps this helps explain the conflict between British "political studies" and American "political science," between the stress on "teaching" in the small ivy colleges and on "research" in land-grant universities, between soft and hard writing, and finally between the relaxed manners of the older orders and the uncouth arrogance of the *nouveau riches*.

None of these casual impressions, of course, have anything to do with the merits of approaches to understanding political phenomena. They might, however, make us sensitive to some gains and losses. Critics of a behavioral social science—self-styled humanists—have failed to see the positive benefits of having simply more individuals become active participants in a collective pursuit and for getting more resources for scholarship generally. They have criticized behavioralists not for being insufficiently empirical but for the triviality of their conclusions and the gracelessness of their writing.[2] They have scarcely criticized the emergence of new closures. Thus the old guard has raised few questions about a model for research which regards a developed polity in terms of system maintenance rather

[2] Becoming preoccupied by methodologies, conceptual problems, and protocol statements, behavioralists may change their style. As conclusions turn out to be the less interesting parts of behavioral reports, what should hold our interest is the disciplined ingenuity with which a question is raised, a moral impulse repressed, seemingly random behavior integrated, and previous work studiously ignored or gratefully acknowledged.

than in terms of its capacity for satisfying a greater variety of interests, needs, and values. It has scarcely been noted how the prevailing approach fails to incorporate latent values and disorganized interests at the periphery or outside of "the political system," how it fails to account for phenomena of potential political value, how it rejects as "dysfunctional" whatever is too weak to be manifest in political life.

In much of what today goes under the name of a science of politics, such elusive phenomena are neither represented nor given opportunities to present themselves. Men who do not express their feelings—or decisions that do not get made—remain invisible. Potentialities may be given a place in novels or films, but for the disciplined political scientist they are incomprehensible. When he recognizes them at all, he places them off limits.

It is not especially difficult to show in what blunt or subtle ways those who have sought to study political affairs scientifically have imposed their view of what is relevant and introduced fixed boundaries—first, it is true, as hypotheses, but ultimately as conclusions.[3] The theories of

[3] An extensive bibliographical footnote of the growing body of widely scattered criticism may be helpful: Thomas J. Anton, "Power, Pluralism, and Local Politics," *Administrative Science Quarterly*, 7 (March, 1963), 425-57, and correspondence (December, 1963), 250-68; Peter Bachrach and Morton S. Baratz, "Two Faces of Power," *American Political Science Review*, 56 (December, 1962), 947-52; Christian Bay, "Politics and Pseudopolitics: A Critical Evaluation of Some Behavioral Literature," *American Political Science Review*, 59 (March, 1965), 39-51; and "The Cheerful Science of Dismal Politics," in Theodore Roszak (ed.), *The Dissenting Academy* (New York: Pantheon Books, 1968); William E. Connolly, *Political Science and Ideology* (New York: Atherton Press, 1967); Bernard Crick, *The American Science of Politics* (Berkeley: University of California Press, 1959), Chap. 7; Lane Davis, "The Cost of Realism: Contemporary Restatements of Democracy," *Western Political Quarterly*, 17 (March, 1964), 37-46; Maure L. Goldschmidt, "Democratic Theory and Contemporary

checks and balances, of American political pluralism, of anti-ideological politics, of the U.S. party system, and of federalism might all have been useful postulates, provisionally offered and subject to empirical inquiry. But boundaries adopted for analytical purposes have tacitly been converted into barricades.

As political scientists testify that a prevailing system "works" (being American, natural, functional, viable, stable, healthy, etc.), they free themselves for the task of characterizing the functions of the system. Thus they can be "objective" in identifying apathy, nonparticipation, role confinement, the privatization of life, or arrested political development as functions of a well-working system. An introduction to an anthology on American politics (to use examples which called for no extensive research) can innocently claim that "everything in this book concerns what is, not what ought to be" while a case study of the American

---

Political Science," *Western Political Quarterly*, 19 (September, 1966), supplement, 5-12; Norman Jacobson, "Political Science and Political Education," *American Political Science Review*, 57 (September, 1963), 561-69; K. W. Kim, "The Limits of Behavioral Explanation in Politics," *Canadian Journal of Economics and Political Science*, 31 (August, 1964), 315-27; Grant McConnell, *Private Power and American Democracy* (New York: Alfred A. Knopf, 1966), Chap. 10; Alasdair MacIntyre, "Breaking the Chains of Reason," in E. P. Thompson *et al.*, *Out of Apathy* (London: Stevens, 1960), pp. 195-240; Herbert Marcuse, *One Dimensional Man* (Boston: Beacon Press, 1964), pp. 113-18; P. H. Partridge, "Politics, Philosophy, Ideology," *Political Studies*, 9 (October, 1961), 217-35; Charles Perrow, "The Sociological Perspective and Political Pluralism," *Social Research*, 31 (Winter, 1964), 412-22; James Petras, "Ideology and United States Political Scientists," *Science and Society*, 29 (Spring, 1965), 192-216; Jack L. Walker, "A Critique of the Elitist Theory of Democracy," *American Political Science Review*, 60 (June, 1966), 285-95; and Robert Paul Wolff *et al.*, *A Critique of Pure Tolerance* (Boston: Beacon Press, 1965), Chap. 1. I have tried to show how the ideology of pluralism permeates and constrains contemporary political research in my *Decline of American Pluralism* (Stanford: Stanford University Press, 1961), Chap. 9; and in "Pluralism," *International Encyclopedia of the Social Sciences* (New York: Macmillan, 1968).

political process can conclude: "One thing about the American governmental process, however, has amazed many generations of students. Somehow it works."[4] These are small slips, and more guarded language might have kept them from being obvious and quotable. Had the authors been less concerned with writing lively prose or with making dreary reports engaging, they may have been able to conceal their values, and one would have to cut deeper to expose them. Thus the fallacy of closure is less apparent when the political scientist simply expects his readers to share his values—his concern for what *is*—and proceeds to construct a general theory of the political system and its development. He closes alternatives the moment he treats immediately observable reality as the only one. Assuming what is real to be "out there," believing that the only problem is to describe it, his focus is then not on what might *conceivably* be observed, not on what moral categories and experimental action might yet establish, but rather on what *is*.

The mode of analysis which leads to such "realism" has become commonplace. A set of relationships is identified as the "political system" and subjected to factor analysis: the political scientist inquires how discrete components within the system function in relation to what he regards as the whole. The components may be normative (such as "values"), legal (such as a constitution), economic (the means of production), psychological (child rearing), or perhaps

[4] Raymond E. Wolfinger (ed.), *Readings in American Political Behavior* (Englewood Cliffs, N.J.: Prentice-Hall, 1966), pp. vii-viii; Clyde E. Jacobs and John F. Gallagher, *The Selective Service Act* (New York: Dodd, Mead, 1967), p. 204. There is no scarcity of examples in political science introductory course texts.

geographic (climate). But whatever components are examined, they are assumed to be embedded within the boundaries of the system under study.

There is so much consensus about the location of a political system's boundaries that it has become easy to assume they have drawn themselves, quite independent of our choices. For analytical purposes, a political system is simply assumed to exist, its components in dynamic interaction. There would seem to be no problem as to what functions make a system a *political* one. No standard external to it, no norm of legitimacy, is imposed. Because the question about functions is addressed to the system itself, the answer, not surprisingly, turns out to be self-maintenance—which means maintenance of the relationships duly established within it. Institutions which are familiar—which the powerful have *made* familiar—are simply accepted. Why should political scientists conceive of competing institutions which might function differently? Who would profit and who would lose if they inquired whether the function of a political system might be something other than self-maintenance? Who is appeased by the prevailing form of analysis?

Identifying part of reality as a system, characterizing it as functional, and designating it as "real," the political scientist, whatever his intent, in effect responds to the call of established elites. So-called systems theory is thus attached to the dominant groups of society, to the definition of law and order accepted by the powerful. Still following nineteenth-century sociological positivism, such a science venerates history definitively understood and classified. It celebrates power and success and stability.

Gabriel Almond's procedure for confirming the location

of system boundaries is a case in point.[5] He assuredly does not proceed to draw his boundaries recklessly, innocent of the fallacy of closure. Yet while confessing to his hesitancies, recognizing the arrogance of presuming "objectively" to fix the boundaries of a political system, he nonetheless affirms that there *are* boundaries, and that these can after all be located: "A system starts somewhere," he writes smoothly, "and stops somewhere." Why should there be any real difficulty in deciding *where?* He disarmingly asks us to consider how relatively easy it is to draw boundaries when we deal with machines or organisms.

But is it? We are said to be altogether certain, to use his illustration, where the automobile ends and the highway (or the driver) begins. Yet have we not made some prior decision about the function of a machine (or an organism)? Such a decision is scarcely seen as boundary fixing when there is an unchallenged consensus on the function of a system: we are all dead-certain about the function of an automobile in relation, for example, to the driver's economic or psychological needs. We can therefore unhesitatingly treat the machine as a system. Even more, we can simply say it *is* a system. Don't we know what a car is for, what its purpose is? It would be absurd to maintain (or would it?) that the function of a car is to maintain the accident rate at its present level. Given a car's *real* purpose, and assuming it to have no others, we can readily specify in what ways it is functional or dysfunctional. The difficulty arises, of course, the moment we deal with a system which has been less persuasively advertised than our transportation system. It arises when a system makes us somehow uneasy

[5] "A Developmental Approach to Political Systems," *World Politics*, 17 (January, 1965), 183-214.

—as every existing *political* system does. Because the purpose of a political system is not given or agreed upon we remain hesitant and remind ourselves, as Almond reminds himself, that we must use guarded language. We know that viability (which may also be called success, power, survival, or stability) is not the only purpose of a political system, if indeed it is the central purpose of a political system at all. True, viability may be the only thing we mention when we feel all is well and ideological conflict has ended. But there are always troublemakers who insist that our successes are also failures, that a good deal which survives is outrageous, that just possibly it is *not* absurd to maintain that the political system is designed to maintain the accident rate at its present level. If we have such suspicions, we must not only be hesitant before drawing boundaries around a political system, congratulating ourselves on our scientific rectitude; we must also refrain from drawing them so that what lies inside will be framed once and for all. We cannot permit ourselves to imply that it has at long last become possible to specify the function of a man-made system in unambiguous, definitive terms.

It is true that Almond's analysis allows for a system's prospective capabilities (just as David Truman's analysis of American pluralism was generous enough to tolerate potential interest groups). But this is at best fine rhetoric, a concession which remains empty as long as actual research commitments preclude the experimentation required to create a new range of capabilities.[6] Systems theory effectively shields us against instability and risk, against disorder and

[6] What Almond concedes he may also take back: he says that he uses the concept of capability to characterize performance (*op. cit.*, pp. 96, 204-205).

violence, against the cost of supporting outsiders who might enter, against the introduction of politics into unfamiliar tracts of our lives. What Bay has called the cheerful science of dismal politics thereby keeps us from gaining knowledge of a potential political reality, of our unused capabilities for development.

There have of course been persistent efforts to overcome such closure. The example of Arthur F. Bentley's *The Process of Government* (1908) and *Behavior, Knowledge, Fact* (1935) seems to me most relevant here, for it also reveals the difficulties of accepting what I think are the significant dimensions of his approach. Several years ago, Norman Jacobson made exactly this point, noting how little honor we have done Bentley—or more precisely how little of Bentley we have honored.[7] Bentley wished to be done with the kind of causal analysis by which behavior is traced to feelings, ideals, motives, instincts, or faculties. Going further, he in fact challenged the very notion of causality. For him, as Jacobson was to put it, all was movement and flux, all was process. He rejected every form of determinism in favor of undifferentiated process. He wanted social life stated exclusively in terms of activity—stated, not explained. The objective—impossible to reach—was to comprehend the whole, to let no part of political reality be confused with the whole, to let no cluster of specific words finally stand for political reality.

Programmatically, Bentley failed: those who followed him became preoccupied by his discussion of groups rather than by his case for seeing political life as process. They as-

[7] "Causality and Time in Political Process," *American Political Science Review*, 58 (March, 1964), 15-22.

pired to build a science of politics, not to destroy analytical approaches to the world. Where Bentley had been destructive, legions of group theorists and system analysts resolved to become constructive. Giving him credit for his concern with groups, carefully dating him, they failed to confront his more basic case for a new style. They used his subject matter, not his form. They failed to see that Bentley remains valuable not because he developed a tool for measuring the flow of pressure in politics (although that is what he talked about) but because of his own defiant style, his obstinate stance, his maddening idiom. His queer way of presenting himself remains finally as the most durable part of his work, so that whatever may be the fate of group analysis and system theory, Bentley's shrill affirmation of life as process remains in the end.

It is necessary to add, I think, that as Bentley assented to life as process, he did not mystically dissolve in it. However nihilistic the tendency of his work, he was never merely "discharging" or "releasing" or "falling free." The very ambiguity of his language—the prose political scientists were to ignore because it seemed incomprehensible—kept the world from closing in on him. Retaining his balance between the concrete and the abstract, Bentley did not succumb to the romantic notion that all language must congeal life. He kept using language. His passionate determination to stay in touch and keep communicating, his use of the conventions of the community, shows him to accept grammar, order, structure, discipline—all tokens of death. But these very restraints—his books—contributed to the fullness of his life. The question is therefore not whether Bentley was for process and against order but to what extent his work succeeds in dramatizing the tension between them.

Whatever chaotic process Bentley saw "out there" he tried somehow to be sympathetic to it, to save it, and yet to give it a measure of order. He buoyantly proclaimed (as Jacobson quotes him) that "the continents go, and the islands." *But the words remained afloat*, and it was not Bentley's fault that some of them were to be seized to analyze American politics so as to dismiss all idealism and rationalize the prevailing group struggle. If, then, our sleep is still unbroken, it was not for lack of Bentley's trying but for the perverse success of his self-selected followers. Whatever continents and islands they have settled for, the thrust of Bentley's thinking and the style of his argument pointed to no settlement whatever. He drew no conclusions.

Yearning for meaning in an America where so much is waste and spoils, where the realized dream of the successful is the nightmare of the failures, we have not been able to keep ourselves from drawing conclusions. We have proceeded to fix the boundary between our political system and what is presumed to be the desert beyond. Presuming to know where to draw the boundary, we have scarcely recognized that quality in traditional political inquiry which remains irritatingly subversive—not, of course, the conclusions of political philosophers, not the developed conceptual systems of Plato or Hegel, but the sheer fact of their writing and communicating. Our blindness to our own need to *continue* philosophizing is shown by our inability to perceive that nothing is as radical in the Platonic dialogues, for example, as their author's often wearisome inconclusiveness. Like other great dramatists, he admittedly did have his closure problem: his voice is not always tentative. But we should realize that his work challenges our desire to be done with talking. It challenges the belief that the relevant facts will someday be in. The usual interpretation to the contrary, there is no expectation that in the end, if only we were diligent and ingenious enough, all variables might finally be related and utopia be established. And what is true of our view of Plato is surely no less true of our view of acknowledged empiricists like Hobbes and Bentham who, it is mistakenly said, will have us settle for the coldest of reason and the best of English common sense. Again, it is our interest in conclusions which makes us overlook that they made their case in a manner so impassioned and extravagant that their very style systematically qualifies their explicit points.

The empirical temper, as Bentley's work demonstrates, demands more of us than finding refuge in palpable reality and appreciating that small part of the American scene which is mature and responsible and democratic. It demands accepting a romantic activism manifest in an eagerness to cut through the first order of appearances, then on to the second, interminably questing (like Plato's Socrates) for an ever-receding, never-established reality. We may of course decide to rest, as many have today, mandarins infatuated by methodologies. We may relax and falsely identify reality with what we have so expertly placed "out there": the institutions identified by the predicates of our sentences. But to tolerate such exhaustion is to compromise that openness to possibilities characteristic of the empirical temper.

I do not mean to suggest that empiricism is generally extinguished today, that authentic political philosophy is dead. Writers as diverse as Norman O. Brown, Herbert Marcuse, R. D. Laing, Norman Mailer, Hannah Arendt, and Francis Golffing have all attempted to deprive us of finalities and reifications. All have struggled against closure. They have desperately sought to avoid giving us some positive vision, some impregnable alternative. They have found themselves engaged in a gigantic housecleaning.[8] Unwilling to make firm distinctions and counsel direct action, unwilling to reorganize our actual experience, they have yet rejected what we like to call reality. Eloquently refraining from making a case for a "better" reality to be enclosed by new boundaries, they have been impelled (as Nietzsche was) toward a final state of silence. Unnerved by the obscenities of this century, they have sketched out no utopias. Beginnings have not seemed justifiable: there is too much knowledge of good and evil, an excess of awareness of the horror which has come from action based on functional rationality, on a science of means. If they exemplify a tradition, it is merely because they keep the possibility of philosophizing alive, thus providing (barely providing) a basis for men not as victims of dead forms but as actors free to design the conventions by which to live. Although not at home in the

---

[8] This negativism is striking today in all the arts. It is patronizingly described by Irving Howe, "The Culture of Modernism," *Commentary*, November 1967, pp. 48-59. Perhaps it is most easily discussed in reference to the novels of Alain Robbe-Grillet. He writes, as Frank Kermode has commented, so that "the reader will find none of the gratification to be had from sham causality, falsely certain description, clear story. The new novel 'repeats itself, bisects itself, modifies itself, contradicts itself, without ever accumulating enough bulk to constitute a past—and thus a "story," in the traditional sense of the word.' The reader is not offered easy satisfactions, but a challenge to creative co-operation. . . . Rival versions of the same set of facts can co-exist without final reconciliation." Violating temporality, chronology, and successiveness, Robbe-Grillet has the same character murdered four times over, which, as Kermode observes, is "certainly a shrewd blow at paradigmatic expectations." (Kermode, *The Sense of an Ending: Studies in the Theory of Fiction* [New York: Oxford University Press, 1967], pp. 19-21). Even poetry which seems as closed as that of T. S. Eliot may be read as an attack on established literature. (*See* Richard Poirier, "T. S. Eliot and the Literature of Waste," *The New Republic*, May 20, 1967, 19-26.)

political science departments of our universities, they have been the unacknowledged custodians of political science as an open-ended system.

One relevant writer is R. D. Laing, whose *Politics of Experience* (1967) is a furious assault on the concept of normality, a desperate case for dissolving the ego by drugs, by direct experience, by and in violence, thereby to affirm the awesome emptiness at the center of man. Laing argues for a divorce from all foundations, for severance and dissolution, hoping (unlike D. H. Lawrence, he is too breathless to say so) that in the end some holy, healthy rebirth may take place. Never pausing to inquire how men might find the psychological strength to establish themselves, how they might act without ontological security, Laing nevertheless induces us to share his vision of the present as sterile, impersonal, meaningless—as radically unpolitical.

It is Norman O. Brown's work, I think, which reveals most clearly what is involved today in a thoroughgoing attack not only on conventional forms but on all forms. His *Love's Body* (originally meant to be entitled "The Body Politic") shows how impossible it is for us to share what I take to be his positive vision, and how rewarding it nonetheless is to watch him put on his hopeless act. The very form of the book exposes his contempt for orderly research, scholarship, and science.[9] His overwrought, filigreed work shocks us into recognizing how incapable *we* are of decorating *our* publications. His self-indulgent indifference to logical relationships makes us see how exquisitely disciplined we are. Writing to annihilate reality, he of course depicts it. By rejecting old connections and accept-

---

[9] In this respect it resembles Malraux's *Voices of Silence* (1953).

ing new ones promiscuously, by welcoming accidents and happenings, he shows us how betrayed we are by our civilization and law, by our walls and barriers, our grotesque division of labor. He makes us aware of the fragmentation of our thought and our action. By nature, so his work intones, man is One; by a kind of self-betrayal, man has become divided and now confuses the parts with the whole. Pushing everything to its extreme, enlisting T. W. Adorno to note that "only the exaggerations are true," Brown seeks to destroy history (at least the history we are made to recall), our symbolization of the past, our unavoidable distortions, the myths which coerce us. He finally seeks to disarm utterly: "The conclusion of the whole matter is," he writes, "break down the boundaries, the walls. Down with defense mechanisms, character-armor; disarmament. . . ."[10] As we hold his book, weighing it, we wonder if there could properly be anything more, anything in addition to type, paper, glue, and a hard cover. *This* seems to be the last weapon, all we are armed with in the end. Because his one bit of explicitly constructive advice—to commence building a heaven in our hell, to create an erotic reality—must strike us as wholly unhinged from possibilities, all we have (all being said and done) is the physical book.

Still, Brown compels us to become aware of our repressions, our divided selves, our limited, distinctive identities. We need not take his program for the obliteration of all distinctions seriously—not even his marvelous solution to the problem of identity (if you can't find yourself, he says, "get lost"). But we can take seriously the need to open the windows and clean house. Exuberantly displaying life as undifferentiated reality, he does make us conscious of our

[10] Norman O. Brown, *Love's Body* (New York: Random House, 1966), p. 149.

own cluttered intellectual edifices, our accumulations, our property. If he gets away with Nothing, might we not get away with something?

As we seek to maintain political science as an open-ended system, to break through established boundaries and invade the wilderness beyond certified "reality," our problem is to keep from constructing a new set of permanent installations. New destinations and new communities will have to be defined so ambivalently that they cannot possibly become new fetishes.

Our point of departure must of necessity be what we experience as "real"—the ideas and institutions we know to be present and accounted for, here and now. We must begin with the very "facts" (as we call them) which circumscribe our vision and keep us in our place. This requires relating fully to them, approaching them with openness and sympathy, letting them *be*—indeed, encouraging them to be. Thus Kurt Wolff has argued for "surrender," by which he means

> total involvement, suspension of received notions, pertinence of everything, identification, risk of being hurt. To "surrender" means to take as fully, to meet as immediately, as possible: *not* to select, *not* to believe that one can know quickly what is to be understood and acted on, hence what one's experience means, *not* to suppose that one can do justice to the experience with one's received feeling and thinking, even with the received *structure* of that feeling and thinking; to meet it as much as possible in its originality, its itself-ness.[11]

[11] Kurt H. Wolff, "Beginning: In Hegel and Today," in Wolff and Barrington Moore, Jr. (eds.), *The Critical Spirit: Essays in Honor of Herbert Marcuse* (Boston: Beacon Press, 1967), p. 96. When one surrenders, Wolff adds, one catches something—something one couldn't anticipate catching; moreover, one's harvest "always is a new conceiving, a new concept, a new beginning, a new being-in-the-world." Hence one's role is feminine. (*See* also the works cited by Wolff, note 1.)

Such empathy with reality—ultimately with the totality of being—is hard to muster, for the very existence of what we confront dismays us. We are disconcerted by what is manifestly established: its mere success rankles. We find it hard to support institutions which impinge on us; we feel impelled to remind their defenders that they are mere partisans, unenlightened possessors of only partial truths. It is hard to suspend judgment, *not* to impose one's own more capacious vision of possibilities. Yet unless we restrain our aggressive impulses, our impulse to frame reality and depict it in terms we impose, we cannot bring unstructured or differently structured human potentialities out into the open. To explain phenomena in their own terms they must be depicted without condescension, not as signs, functions, or symptoms but as expressions of whatever presumes to exist.

Although we may speak, as I just have, of explaining things "in their own terms," I realize, of course, that this is impossible. To explain is necessarily to abstract and compare; it is to use words which relate similar aspects of diverse phenomena. Nevertheless, we can aim as Norman Mailer did in *Armies of the Night* (1968), to minimize abstraction, to move as close to the phenomena as we can without losing ourselves. To make well-protected private matters public—to make them known—we must seek to balance self-conscious detachment with selfless attachment.

The difficulties of this strategy are undeniable. How hard it is to accommodate phenomena and let them be themselves is exhibited in the intellectual career of Karl Mannheim. To understand the society of his day, Mannheim had urged that social scientists identify with social reality and partake in group action. They were to let themselves become involved in ideological warfare; they were to help give expression to the prevailing beliefs in the clearest, most coherent fashion. By doing so, Mannheim believed, it would become possible for them to comprehend social forces which had remained unexpressed, to display the realities of power embedded in the historical process. They would gain knowledge by becoming sympathetic to the course of history, getting in step with it, marching wherever it might go, and making periodic progress reports. But by the time Hitler came to power, Mannheim changed his mind. We are not bemused by matters of life and death. The new order Hitler had inspired proved to be intolerable. The method of "Verstehen" was well and good as long as rationality seemed to govern the process of history and left the future indeterminate. In view of the barbarism of the Nazi regime, however, the historical process had to be resisted. A trans-historical standard—one not implicit in the events of the day—had to be applied so as to condemn and oppose forces of history which threatened an open future and had every chance of success. As judgment became unavoidable for Mannheim, the limits of sympathy were exposed.

We now know that Mannheim was right in drawing the line where he did. But there was no certain way of predicting when serious resistance would be imperative as well as possible, just as there is no telling today to what extent the forces now at loose in the world are properly approached with ambivalence, in an ironical manner. How can we tell which contemporary movements are likely to destroy the very possibility of rational action, civil discourse, speculative inquiry, and social science? How can we tell which movements present a clear and present danger to open-ended systems, its members not only threatening closure but having the will and the power to carry out the threat? Our problem is making a sound practical estimate. We may overestimate the threat of direct-action movements, their spontaneity having made us anxious. We are then likely to meet them not on their terms but on ours. No longer caring to comprehend them, we will then seek to neutralize their power. On the other hand we may complacently or naively underestimate the threat they pose, become understanding and forgiving, and help them along. Overestimating them, we may kill them needlessly; underestimating them, we may become their captives. Because we are rather safe than sorry, we prefer the first estimate to the second, forgetting that our growth is arrested in either case.

To enable us to make sound practical estimates, empirical social science would seem to be indispensable. It certainly is the most reliable and precise instrument for indicating under what conditions thoroughgoing empathy is defensible. It can disclose to what extent we are fixed, unable to escape the forces impinging on us, and to what extent we are free to maneuver, to move frivolously in all directions. When the evidence shows us to be located at either pole—within either a structured or an unstructured environment—the case for empathy should be apparent. When our fate is determined, all that is left us is to do in full consciousness what we must do in any event. Disapproval would then be irrelevant and sentimental, there being no feasible alternatives. As long as our efforts to restructure reality are decisively punished, an approving irony is our last resource. When our fate remains quite indeterminate, however, no harm can come from collaborating with the benign processes of history: in a totally permissive, open-ended system, we can freely suspend judgment.

Admittedly, these extremes are fictions; furthermore, we find ourselves in relatively closed environments during one part of the day and relatively open ones during another. Thus discrimination would always seem to be called for: the time and place for unmitigated empathic involvement is necessarily limited. But to the extent that all exits are closed, such involvement is called for and requires no apology.

No doubt, ironic performances in which we relate to the world sympathetically tend to leave a bad taste. If the ironist is free to say yes, why doesn't he use what freedom he has to say no? If he is tormented, why doesn't he at least assert himself and turn on his torturer? We raise these questions, I think, because his and our estimate of his situation differ, because we reject his practical judgment. We are contemptuous of him when we believe (rightly or wrongly) that the time and place for irony had not arrived: he responded ironically under circumstances which in our judgment still allowed him to take action. We believe a stand was not only imperative but also possible, and that he should have taken it upon himself to act and rearrange the world in which he found himself. We might concede that irony may be a justifiable response to terminal disease, a world so sick that it is clearly beyond help, the electric chair, an extermination camp, or an autonomous legislative body whose power is wholly arbitrary. But an ironic response to these situations strikes us as outrageous when we simply do not see them as their victims do, that is, when our empirical estimates differ from theirs.

We can, it is true, esteem the person who, sick unto death, mocks his illness, asserts it does him good, and responds to inquiries about his condition with, "I'm feeling great." Putting on an ironic act, he pretends (to our relief) that all is well, really. Governing his feelings, he continues within the community of the living. He remains an integrated personality in control of himself, not the victim of his pain, his misery, his opiates, or his keepers. As we reflect on his situation, and see its hopelessness, we admit the appropriateness of simulation and irony.

But what if we believe the situation is *not* hopeless, that he might not only control his feelings but also, by an act of will, eradicate the painful condition which gives rise to them? My point, of course, is that the ironic detachment which encourages the world to *be* is proper insofar as our experience warrants either an unreserved optimism or an unreserved pessimism. If we still fail to appreciate the place of irony, perhaps this is because of our distance from extreme situations—a paucity of imagination or a lack of experience. In any case, once empirical estimates confirm that all that remains to us is irony (or, alternatively, that we can safely risk irony because the world is so fluid that we may idly play with it), we may well be ironical with confidence.

Since our situation—personal as well as global—may be both more hopeful and more hopeless than we generally believe it to be, I should like briefly to reflect on the uses of irony and attempt to place it within the system of contemporary political science. I would begin by having us recognize how precariously irony balances detachment and attachment, how it entails an attitude toward phenomena which simultaneously depreciates and appreciates them, and how it demands both a sympathy for actors in the process of history and a scrupulous neutrality toward them. It demands that the observer be removed from his data, and yet be capable of identifying with them in all their specificity.

From the detached vantage point of the ironic observer, those under observation will always appear curiously fond of their specific settings. His distance makes him perceive their innocent partiality—their foibles, limitations, distortions, illusions, their ludicrous conviction that their limited existence is the whole of it. His voice, whether it is that of Weber, Veblen, Riesman, Lasswell, or Galbraith, is passive. Apparently having no interest other than in lucidity, he expects no resolution of the tensions he perceives. He embraces no final substantive good. His approach, as Harold Kaplan has pointed out in a study of contemporary novelists, has a rather special quality: "not really to laugh, not really to weep, nor to cry out in anger or hatred, but to be released from a commitment to action . . . and to transcend all human limitations simply by acknowledging them."[12]

Kaplan has shrewdly seen the appetite for power, the sadistic note, in the search for knowledge of the limitations of others. Irony leads us to perceive others as pathetically captivated by their immediate context, as enmeshed within a process, an historical situation, a field of forces. We see them as submerged, struggling, reduced to movement, objects less free to act than they believe. Irony keeps us detached from them; it allows us to display the cool indifference of a secure elite. Negating and disowning, irony

[12] Harold Kaplan, *The Passive Voice* (Athens, Ohio: Ohio University Press, 1966), p. 27.

puts others—whether the American voter or the objects of Dr. Kinsey's curiosity—in the wider setting visible only to us, and this wider setting invariably qualifies whatever claims *they* may have. It disallows their claims, discounts their ideals, puts whatever is said and done in a comic light. It is patronizing, mocking, derisive, humiliating. Its posture has been portrayed by Bertolt Brecht, who wrote "Concerning Poor B. B.":

> I gather some fellows around me towards evening:
> We address each other as "gentlemen."
> They put their feet up on my table
> And say: things will improve. And I don't ask when.

For Brecht's cronies—"gentlemen" who put their feet on the table—it is the end of the day, and all is deflated, as all was deflated by Brecht, as he permitted nothing but his words to come out clear and true, neither the Free World nor the Communist Party, neither science nor drama. For irony, there are no warm affirmations or heated rejections, only a Socratic impartiality which frames contradictory ideals while it relieves us from judgment—and ultimately from the action which judgment calls for. Not presuming to prescribe, it merely makes explicit.

Its effect has been made vivid by Bergson:

> Try, for a moment, to become interested in everything that is being said and done; act, in imagination, with those who act, and feel with those who feel; in a word give your sympathy its widest expansion; as though at the touch of a fairy wand you will see the flimsiest of objects assume importance, and a gloomy hue spread over everything. Now step aside, look upon life as in disinterested speculation: many a drama will turn into a comedy.

To produce the whole of its effect, then, the comic demands

something like a momentary anesthesia of the heart. Its appeal is to intelligence, pure and simple.[13]

Anesthetizing the heart, we can see the historical actors as they see themselves—but more fully. We can bear to look, as they cannot. Beholding them beneath us, we can trace their movements and note implications to which they are blind. We can think aloud where men are silent, representing them in tribunals—our own elevated ones—in which they are absent.

As we tease out implications, we gradually perceive the ambiguity of all language. The words men use ultimately direct us to their very opposites, leading us to see how every victorious word implies a defeat. Our analytical procedure can therefore recall what has been defeated, saving obliterated and unrealized interests, demonstrating that at least in the world of symbols no victories need be final. How this analytical activity works has been shown by Kenneth Burke:

> Terms have implications; they suggest other terms, and other things named by those terms. In sum, they suggest all sorts of further possibilities, a logic of future development beyond the present situations.
>
> In the broadest sense, such a profusion and development of implications is to be seen in religious and political doctrines that hold out various kinds of promises to those who accept the logic of their implication and enroll in their name. But this process works in many ways less obvious though equally provocative.
>
> If a writer happens to imagine a likely character in a likely situation, this much of a theme can suggest many other devel-

[13] Henri Bergson, *Laughter* (New York: Macmillan, 1921), pp. 4-5 (quoted by Kaplan, *op. cit.*).

opments in keeping with it. He may gradually work up a whole set of characters, all variously designed to throw light upon the character with which he started or to help develop the original situation into a plot. Thus, to get such a germ for a story is to become excited by a sense of futurity centering in more or less clearly developed ideas about the possibilities which the project implies. And the further our writer goes in developing his theme, the more compulsive his attachment to it is likely to become. He "must" finish his book; he "must" carry these possibilities to their perfection.

Such a responsiveness to implications seems to be at the bottom of all our human enterprises, based as they are on our nature as word-using, symbol-using animals. We are inherently endowed with terminologies that imply many sorts of potentialities and thus *goad* us to plan for their actualization.[14]

The very act of writing, it should be clear, induces the writer to identify a previously unknown reality. He does not quite know what he will be doing until he has done it. It is in the act itself that his work is created: the activity *is* the work. Assuming no prefigured end, we can acclaim him not for his end-result but for his capacity for managing the diversities of relevant experience.

Not surprisingly, such activity will be attacked as "nihilistic" and "relativistic." Thus Leo Strauss has lamented its promiscuity: it is open to everything human—and ultimately succumbs to everything human. According to Strauss, critical judgment is not only suspended: it is altogether eliminated. All positions turn out to be equally true. And this is moral chaos.[15] However, it is far from clear, despite Strauss's claim, why the social scientist (or the nov-

[14] Kenneth Burke, "Motion, Action, Words," *Teachers College Record*, 62 (December, 1960), 245-46.

[15] "Social Science and Humanism," in Leonard D. White (ed.), *The State of the Social Sciences* (Chicago: University of Chicago Press, 1956), pp. 415-25.

elist, for that matter) is morally disarmed by the method of irony. Irony, like skepticism, implies a last-ditch moral commitment to the enhancement of experience. Thus Richard Hoggart has shown how the artist, beginning with his most immediate concerns, is morally driven to broaden the range of his experience, cherishing dimensions of life not previously felt to be significant:

> Literature . . . starts in an absorbed attention to the "thisness" of experience, in an immersion in "the destructive element," in "the foul rag and bone shop of the heart." It, first, *celebrates* all this—"blesses . . . what there is for being." It works not by precept and abstraction but by dramatization, by "showing forth," by creating the "felt sense of life" in its complicated fullness—of sense and feeling and thought, of time and place and persons. In ordering its dramas it is driven by a desire to find Theseus' thread, the moment of epiphany, the revelatory instance, the tiny gesture that opens a whole field of meaning and consequence. It does not do this "playfully"—it really *is* concerned with meanings here; but it does not do this so as to reform, either; it does so, I think first for the extraordinary momentary peace of knowing that a little more of the shifting amorphousness of experience has been named and held, that we are now that bit less shaken by the anarchy of feeling and the barbarous assault of experience, that we are that much less likely (to combine two quotations) to be blown about the pendant world, in fractured atoms.

But to push for this kind of truth, no matter how much it may hurt, is a kind of moral activity. I am glad to quote Jung (rather than a literary critic) on the work of a poet: "[He] forces the reader to greater clarity and depth of human insight by bringing fully into his consciousness what he ordinarily evades or overlooks or senses only with a feeling of dull discomfort."[16]

---

[16] Richard Hoggart, "Schools of English and Contemporary Society," *American Scholar*, 33 (Spring, 1964), 241.

To engage in the activity delineated by Hoggart, we must express ourselves dialectically and discursively, offering denials after each of our affirmations, multiplying our meanings, exploding our reifications. The appropriate style is unavoidably "literary," for our conclusions are found not at the end but in the totality of the work. Attempting to describe, drawing out what is entailed, we subvert immediate reality by revealing complexities and finally alternatives. Our discipline—again, Mailer's *Armies of the Night* is a case in point—consists of rigorously attending to the complexity of the data, remaining alert to needless closures. We are disciplined insofar as we resist the temptation to become didactic, refuse to add an explicit moral, and thus decline to end our discourse.

The proper method, as I have indicated, requires first being sensitive to what is said and then driving the prevailing rhetoric to its own logical conclusions, exposing the end to which it leads. Moreover, it is to be attentive to what is done, literally to take note of our behavior, and then to project it into the future, elucidating its probable results. By extrapolating, we help those involved in public life understand what they are doing, making them see the worrisome, unanticipated outcomes of their decisions. "Everything that is thought about a good deal," Nietzsche remarked in his *Thus Spake Zarathrustra*, "is finally thought suspicious." Abstracting and building political models, we make ourselves aware of our conduct, compelling ourselves in the end to act with more concern for alternatives.

This method has been employed by writers as diverse as Weber, Kafka, Schumpeter, Veblen, and Lasswell—all fastidious ironists affectionately clinging to data they abhorred, all seeking to depict our environments so precisely and elaborately that their work was bound to jeopardize the hopes of the successful by altering conventional perceptions. Weber writing on bureaucracy, Kafka on organizational labyrinths, Schumpeter on capitalism, Veblen on our economic conventions, and Lasswell on the garrison state have pointed to dimensions of our public affairs we do not ordinarily perceive. Focusing on our surroundings, these writers have rigorously projected, exposing contexts and consequences, exploring fuller meanings of the prevailing forms. They initially turned (as Tocqueville had done in his day) to what appeared to them most striking in the present, the impulses in society which were upsetting the prevailing balance. They then sought to articulate the patterns, tendencies, potencies, and movements of the age. They in effect anticipated Raymond Williams, who, suspending judgment, decided to give his assent to what he has called the long revolution. The merely *critical* posture, Williams wrote in 1961, has become irrelevant:

> In naming the great process of change in the long revolution, I am trying to learn assent to it, an adequate assent of mind and spirit. I find increasingly that the values and meanings I need are all in this process of change. If it is pointed out in traditional terms, that democracy, industry, and extended communications are all means rather than ends, I reply that this, precisely, is their revolutionary character, and that to realize and accept this requires new ways of thinking and feeling, new conceptions of relationships, which we must try to explore.[17]

It cannot quite go without saying that in order to define the relationships to which Williams wishes to assent, we are well served by empirical science—indeed a positivistic, naturalistic empirical science. There is perhaps no better way

---

[17] Raymond Williams, *The Long Revolution* (New York: Columbia University Press, 1961), p. xiii.

for identifying our limitations, compulsions, fatuities, and addictions—our various nonpolitical enclosures—than by the narrowest of empirical research.[18] At its best, it can reveal how much of our conduct is in fact conditioned, repetitive, and compulsive. Perceiving our behavior, it provides us with empirically confirmed generalizations about the world as it presents itself. Even when empiricists remain naive about their assumptions, when they claim to offer no point of view and presume merely to describe "objectively" what things are "really" like (or, still less plausibly, what things really *are*), they may nonetheless disclose relationships where we believed things to be unrelated, acci-

[18] A positivistic empiricism disregarding man as purposeful actor may be useful precisely because it does *not* presume to focus on distinctively political phenomena. Curiously, this proposition tends to be denied by both those who reject and those who favor positivistic approaches. It is instructive to puzzle out what "politics" must mean to someone who believes that "an adequate explanation of a great many human *actions* can be made with no reference at all to motives, particularly when the individual is acting in a highly structured social situation—*the usual case in much of politics.*" I would submit that behavior can indeed be explained without reference to motives and that it occurs precisely in highly structured situations; but I would also argue that oppressive situations which tolerate no choice are to that extent nonpolitical, and that nonpolitical situations are the very ones amenable to behavioral study. The point simply is that at particular times some men behave and some act—and that one cannot tell who does what merely by looking at them. Similarly, some men intentionally act on the political stage while others just cannot help themselves—and mere observation will not enable us to distinguish between the two types. (The quotation, with my emphasis, is from Eugene J. Meehan, *Contemporary Political Thought* [Homewood, Illinois: Dorsey Press, 1967], p. 81; I have touched on the distinction between action and behavior in "A Comment on Methods," *American Political Science Review*, 54 [March, 1960], 200-201.) The logical impossibility of explaining purposeful action in terms of scientific correlations or such concepts as cause and effect is shown by Richard Taylor, *Action and Purpose* (Englewood Cliffs, N.J.: Prentice-Hall, 1966); *see* also A. R. Louch, *Explanation and Human Action* (Oxford, England: Blackwell, 1966); and John G. Gunnell, "Social Science and Political Reality: The Problem of Explanation," *Social Research*, 35 (Spring 1968), 159-201.

dental, and mysterious. They thereby enable us to observe ourselves more fully.

At times there is in fact no alternative to detached observation. At such times, explicit acquiescence is all that is possible—or necessary. When alternatives are cut off, we may yet save what we can by complying and leaving as much of a record of our compliance as we dare. To be sure, few social scientists exemplify what I have in mind: few have succeeded as brilliantly as Orson Welles, leaving visible traces of their unused surplus talent. Welles' career shows him to have consented to play the roles he was assigned in mediocre films; but being unable to change the economics of the mass entertainment system, he played them as comedy. Too big for his roles (as Pauline Kael has said in a telling review), he used his surfeit of talent "to tell the audience that you know that what you're doing isn't worth doing and still do it better than anyone else in the movie."[19] Perhaps there are times when the pressures on us are so great we can salvage no more. At best and at most, all one can sometimes do is to volunteer to ride our destructive instruments, show our instructors the way by doing well, lead the killers among us, light the fire, direct the revolutions, put ourselves in charge and up front. I realize, of course, that few would wish to add their weight to the weight of the bomb and (like the Texan pilot in "Dr. Strangelove") ride it down cheering, knowing annihilation is unavoidably ahead. But failing to lead *and incapable of providing alternatives*, what choice is there? Failing to contribute, failing to take command, we will be commanded by the powers that be. Why not then give our assent to the

[19] Pauline Kael, "Orson Welles: There Ain't No Way," *The New Republic*, June 24, 1967, p. 67.

unavoidable tendencies of the age, publicly refusing to judge, refusing to say clearly whether we regard them as the worst or the best, as good or evil, knowing only (and, near hysteria, knowing sadly) that they are manifestly there, that they are potentially human and that they can become fully human only if we control them?

"One of the oldest games there is, cat's cradle. Even the Eskimos know it."

"You don't say."

"For maybe a hundred thousand years or more, grownups have been waving tangles of string in their children's faces."

"Um."

Newt remained curled in the chair. He held out his painty hands as though a cat's cradle were strung between them. "No wonder kids grow up crazy. A cat's cradle is nothing but a bunch of X's between somebody's hands, and little kids look and look and look at all those X's . . ."

"And?"

"No damn cat, and no damn cradle."

—Kurt Vonnegut, Jr., *Cat's Cradle* (1963)

FOUR

Political Science as Public Action

When seeking to gain control of a car in a skid by deliberately steering toward disaster, we assume it is too late to escape our fate. We assume we are fully, irreversibly in motion. There is no time and no money to work on better roads, to build less destructive machines, or to train more self-interested drivers. Of course, we seldom find ourselves so helplessly out of control. Nor, for most of us, does the very opposite situation ever apply: few of us are ever free to drive in all directions at will. To the extent, therefore, that in one or another tract of our lives the future is neither quite closed nor quite open, we must reject the ironic posture, oppose reality, and act to establish ourselves. We should then proceed to act on our environment, using it for our purposes; we should then so structure prevailing systems that they will promote our future development. When purposeful action is neither useless nor dispensable, when it is within our power to create meaningful options, we have no warrant for irony. We must then seek to reconceptualize the world about us and to *act* on the basis of our new visions. We should then recall, moreover, that irony is diverting and exhausting, that it dissipates our rage not only when our rage has become useless but also when it might give us the energy to change intolerable conditions. We should then remind ourselves that the witty filigree of irony dissipates our moral power—the power to enlarge one's sympathies. Contradicting the reality to which irony remains attached, we must be prepared to redesign our environment and create new meanings for ourselves.

I am of course merely putting Kant in a contemporary idiom by affirming that *we* design the world of phenomena, that its meaning grows out of our determination to make it yield meaning and out of our power to convert it into something useful. The number of its meanings, in this view, is limited only by the number of uses to which we can put it, the number of experiences we might yet learn to regard as useful, and hence real. It follows that what is really "there" is necessarily a question which no amount of past experience, of confirmed knowledge, can answer.

Because our norms give rise to particular phenomena, they activate the world. The world may well be there, but what we make of it depends on us. This view, it is clear, gives us awesome power, but equally great responsibilities. It should be both encouraging and sobering, I think, to recall the story of the three baseball umpires who were reflecting on how each decided whether a pitch was a ball or a strike. The first one maintained, "I call 'em as they are." The second said, "I call 'em as I see 'em." The third umpire who had obviously been around the longest said, "They aren't nothin' till I call 'em." Our third umpire, it should be evident, knows that without our perception, without our cognitive and evaluative action, phenomena would never make their appearance. We—those of us in power—single out, identify, signify, and illuminate. We call them. Without us as purposeful beings, no events; without the historian, no past.[1] What we single out depends on us—or, more precisely, on the methodological conventions, conceptual frameworks, and boundaries we establish. And since frameworks, dimensions, and boundaries—reality-organizing principles—are man-made, the facts they expose are contingent on what we deem right and proper, on our norms. Our norms, in other words, structure reality. Expressing our dispositions, they dispose over facts—as well as of them. They give reality a significance it cannot otherwise have. Our inquiries, directed by our norms and our conventions, give meaning which reality does not previously possess.

It is purposeful action, accordingly, which provides knowledge. Our knowledge must depend on the questions we raise; our so-called conclusions can have meaning only in reference to the normative designs used to elicit them. We cannot grasp what we are told, cannot understand the

[1] Edward A. Tiryakian has elaborated on the implication of this approach for the historian: "The historian's fundamental endeavor is to make visible anew that present which once was visible but which tends to become invisible once it is engulfed in historical time. The historian, thus, may be properly called the discoverer of the past. The act of historical discovery is one of meaningful perception. . . . For the past to be exhausted as an object would necessarily imply that the future is exhausted, that is, that historical time would no longer have any possibilities of becoming. The ultimate meaning of historical events, therefore, can only be transhistorical, that is, it can only be perceived after all historical possibilities have been actualized and that can only be after there is no more history." ("Sociohistorical Phenomena: The Seen, the Unseen, the Foreseeable," mimeographed paper, prepared for a meeting of the American Historical Association, December, 1966, pp. 8-9.)

meaning of an event, as long as we ignore the trans-historical, normative context in which statements about it are made. Nothing—no one's pitch—can be a ball or a strike until the rules have been specified. Nothing can have meaningful existence until we have agreed on its boundaries. A decision must first have been made on what is legitimately incorporated within them, on what for the moment is real. And since the meaning of reality is not "given," we cannot let the facts lead us to draw the boundaries around reality.

It follows that we might well assume our enclosures—schools, prisons, corporations, bureaucracies—to be more open than past experience indicates, that we should certainly *not* assume them to be as closed as claimed by those who profit by closure and feel secure in the seats of power. Rejecting claims made in behalf of some allegedly sovereign order of facts, we might test existing organizational boundaries, thereby changing them, ideally enlarging the arenas of politics, admitting more of us, satisfying a wider range of human needs.

When we are successful in using what power we have to structure "the facts," when we can make them relevant to our needs, we change boundaries and definitions which have become conventional. Definitions—whether of a "developed" nation or a "mature" individual—are therefore best thought of in terms of our present and future needs, and as immune to invalidation by "the facts," by past experience, or by the "conclusions" of a positivistic empiricism.

Insofar as we have the power to handle the facts, including and excluding them as it suits us, we bestow legitimacy on our boundaries and definitions. Creatively redesigning reality and putting our new designs to the test, we humanize the world we happen to inhabit. We make it valuable.

There is, I would say, no other way of legitimizing our environment, for until the final set of definitions is universally accepted and the last boundary conclusively drawn, until all mortgages are burned and all promises redeemed, there are always more possible experiences men can relate and order. Until nothing further becomes possible—or everything becomes possible at will—a potentially meaningful future still impinges on the present. As long as the future continues to be open—and to the extent that it is open at present—men can draft and enforce the laws of social science: they can theorize and take pains to implement their theories.[2]

Because social scientists have a professional stake in an unattained future, they must perennially regard man's usual business and politics as incomplete ventures. Their concern must be not with specific causes but all conceivable causes. It must be with the partiality of all professed truths and all established parties. The decision on how much reality to encompass and make intelligible is therefore not properly determined by what happens to be "real" at the moment—the experiences now controlled by men now in charge. Which possible order of facts to make visible (and which to leave invisible) must be determined by a standard transcending present constraints.

As we apply our standard, it will inevitably make familiar constraints (for example, a college education) appear incongruous. Constituting a criticism of familiar conditions, it will *change* an accepted state of affairs into a problem. Our standard will make us feel that things are not right, and, when incisively formulated, will finally drive us to put

[2] *See* Alan Gewirth, "Can Men Change Laws of Social Science?" *Philosophy of Science*, 21 (July, 1954), 229-41.

reality to the test. Insofar as we recognize the growth-potential inherent in a situation, doubting the justice of a prevailing balance of forces, we will be impelled to create a new balance.

Our standard cannot be so formulated as to imply that the boundaries we face are fixed; it cannot allow us to believe that our primary intellectual problem is somehow to derive general laws (ultimately causal laws) from the life we now live within the boundaries. It must compel us to see the limits of systemic analysis which seeks to index the present "aggregates of behavior within systems" in order to contribute generalizations to a body of empirical propositions. Our scientific norm will properly induce us to recognize that such generalizations are not about open-ended systems, about men as agents whose options are exhausted by the present, or about purposeful, symbolic action. It will imply, in other words, that there is always something more than immediately describable reality, that there are additional resources, and that these might yet be used to satisfy our need to remain alive to undescribed possibilities.

Consequently what we call "research" must itself be purposeful, directed by our interest in creating options, introducing complexities, complicating our lives, stressing the defects and the excesses of all agreements, ceaselessly qualifying, amending, overturning, and negating. Our scientific operations must insist on imbalance when balance is comforting, and supported by research foundations. They must lead us to see through the things which have been designated "important" and "significant"—not because nothing is finally significant but because the order of significant experiences may be enlarged. We must realize that to demythologize venerable institutions (such as the American high school or the Supreme Court) is not necessarily to annihilate them: it may expose a higher order of complexity.[3]

Thus the prevailing settlements—the existing reality-organizing principles—must always be challenged. None being wholly acceptable, they constitute problems. Our problems, accordingly, are posed not only by an unconquerable reality (for part of reality, when we are empowered to *do* social science, turns out to be conquerable enough) but also by our values, constructs, definitions, methods. Our organizing principles pose a problem precisely to the extent that they do not make reality yield. A survey of public opinion (to use an example few will find persuasive), which does not *change* opinions, which, competing with other mass media, fails to create a new awareness by failing to counteract the existing opinion-molding instruments, constitutes a problem for political science. The norms which direct reality-testing can be regarded as adequate only insofar as they act upon reality, making it more various, compelling powerful men and powerful opinions to yield. Until our concepts and instruments destroy closed orders and move the population into pluralistic, open-ended systems, they remain problematical.

It follows that the problems of political science are ultimately posed by its conceptual frameworks, its methodology. Introductory course lectures notwithstanding, the primary problem is not "discovering" more knowledge about the existing political reality but so to formulate reality-organizing principles that they enable us to know and govern

[3] *See* Arthur Selwyn Miller and Alan W. Scheflin, "The Power of the Supreme Court in the Age of the Positive State: A Preliminary Excursus—Part One: On Candor and the Court, or Why Bamboozle the Natives?" *Duke Law Journal* (1967), 273-320.

a progressively larger reality. The relevant question is how much usable reality our discipline incorporates. How inclusive is it? How successfully does it cope with life's oddities? What is the scope and depth of the experiences on which it touches? How much conflict does it tolerate?[4] We must recognize that values are established by our principles of explanation, our modes of conceptualizing, our research designs, our conventions for verification. These precisely constitute the problem for scientific inquiry. They direct our attention to what is central, notable, note*worthy*—that is, of value.

Since theories function to set limits, none can be presumed to take exhaustive account of reality. They are indispensable for giving meaning, and yet are never adequate. If, then, we wish to multiply meanings, our theories must be ever subject to reformulation. Because we are inclined to relax and accept the prevalent order of things, we must welcome whatever techniques induce us to create new theories. We might, for example, learn to appreciate the way C. Wright Mills used to rearrange his files. He would periodically dump out his manila folders, mixing up their contexts, and then re-sort them. More specifically, supporting a kind of permanent intellectual revolution, he urged:

> An attitude of playfulness toward the phrases and words with which various issues are defined often loosens up the imagination. Look up synonyms for each of your key terms in dictionaries . . . to know the full range of their connotations. . . . Often you get the best insights by considering extremes—by thinking of the opposite of that with which you are directly concerned. If you think about despair, then also think about

[4] These questions are recognized as the relevant ones for the physical sciences by Joseph Schwab, *The Teaching of Science as Enquiry* (Cambridge: Harvard University Press, 1964), p. 39.

> elation; if you study the miser, then also the spendthrift. . . . Let your mind become a moving prism catching light from as many angles as possible. In this connection, the writing of dialogues is often very useful.
> The release of imagination can sometimes be achieved by deliberately inverting your sense of proportions. If something seems very minute, imagine it to be simply enormous, and ask yourself: What difference might it make. . . .[5]

The techniques Mills recommends may be seen, I think, as metaphor for the activity of science. Detaching the imagination from the comfortable theories at hand, they enable us to gain what Kenneth Burke (whom Mills relied on for his strategy) called perspective by incongruity. To free ourselves from our immediate pressures, Burke suggested that we seek dialectically to oppose whatever seems to dictate our fate, attempting to gain knowledge by viewing our situations from incongruous points of view.[6] Using this technique, we might ascribe some disreputable or absurd function to a working social system, inquiring, for example, how the educational system of the high school functions to destroy creativity[7] or how the behavior of the American Medical Association functions to preserve an economic monopoly.[8] Postulating goals contrary to acclaimed ones, we

---

[5] C. Wright Mills, *The Sociological Imagination* (New York: Oxford University Press, 1959), pp. 195-226. *See* also Stuart Hampshire, *Thought and Action* (New York: The Viking Press, 1960), p. 214.

[6] *See* Kenneth Burke, *Attitudes Toward History* (New York: New Republic Books, 1937), Vol. I, p. 213; Vol. II, p. 82. The result of imposing a comic frame on our action would, according to Burke, "not be passiveness, but maximum consciousness." (Vol. I, p. 220.)

[7] *See* Edgar Z. Friedenberg, "The Modern High School: A Profile," in *The Dignity of Youth and Other Atavisms* (Boston: Beacon Press, 1965), pp. 75–95; John R. Seeley, *The Americanization of the Unconscious* (New York: International Science Press, 1967), pp. 338–52.

[8] *See* Reuben A. Kessel, "Price Discrimination in Medicine," *Journal of Law and Economics*, 1 (October, 1958), 20-53.

may be able to explain seemingly queer practices, making sense of them, revealing them to be rational. Thus the corruption of Huey Long's regime might be seen as a wholly rational response to a prevailing system.[9] Alternatively, what is believed to be a sensible, pleasing arrangement, such as capitalism, might be seen as self-contradictory and offensive.

We are likely to hear new voices when we postulate that one or another part of a social system aims at the very reverse of "success," "pacification," "development," "health," or "creativity." We might become sensitive to the anguish inherent in "the merit system" or "gracious living" or "nation building" by negating these phrases, perhaps by enclosing them in quotation marks. Postulating functions which have the effect of shifting our perspectives, we expose previously unseen possibilities. We perceive a new reality—lives *not* lived (or not lived decently) because of decisions *not* made. When the empty space in which potentialities might have been realized is bared, we become aware of our losses.

One approach to such awareness has been sketched out by Peter Bachrach and Morton Baratz.[10] They observe that the student of community power may be blind to the nondemocratic elements of the governing process when he

---

[9] *See* J. S. Nye, "Corruption and Political Development," *American Political Science Review*, 61 (June, 1967), 417-27; Nathaniel H. Leff, "Economic Development through Bureaucratic Corruption," *American Behavioral Scientist*, 8 (November, 1964), 8-14.

[10] "Decisions and Nondecisions: An Analytical Framework," *American Political Science Review*, 57 (September, 1963), 632-42. Also *see* Fowler V. Harper and Alan S. Rosenthal, "What the Supreme Court Did Not Do in the 1949 Term," *University of Pennsylvania Law Review*, 99 (December, 1950), 293-325; the discussion of "influence in repose" in William A. Gamson, *Power and Discontent* (Homewood, Ill.: Dorsey Press, 1968), pp. 93–109; and the remarks by C. Wright Mills, *Power, Politics and People* (New York: Ballantine Books, 1961), p. 23.

focuses on so-called key decisions, that is, on decisions said to be significant. But who, they ask, decides initially what is of significance? Are the issues resolved by key decisions "really" the significant ones? Might elites not be promoting attitudes and practices which confine the scope of democratic decision-making to the formulation of policies not threatening their power? Might elites not be confining democratic participation to issues which, from an undisclosed and undiscussed perspective, would be insignificant—however much they are publicized as *the* key issues first by the elites themselves and subsequently by the students of community power? In that case, the mere fact of democratic participation would not reveal who governs. To learn how power is shared within a community, one would have to inquire whether the power of elites might not also be manifest in what is *not* done. Without developing their idea, Bachrach and Baratz make what I think is a stunning suggestion: social scientists might well investigate the dynamics of nondecision-making.

Yet how could one locate the nonexisting arenas in which nondecision-makers meet and make their nondecisions? After all, those who fail to govern leave no traces and make no noise. Would a behavioral science determined to trace what is visible and record what is audible not be at a loss?[11]

[11] This has been pointed out by K. W. Kim, "The Limits of Behavioral Explanation in Politics," *Canadian Journal of Economics and Political Science*, 31 (August, 1965), 322. Kim suggests that in describing what happened one might also describe how much more happened elsewhere under significantly similar conditions. Or, following Max Weber, one might include "judgments of possibilities." Kim fails to add, however, that we might also *make* things happen, whether in computors, laboratory settings, or society at large. Similarly, William E. Connolly's criticism of C. Wright Mills's propositions as not testable fails to consider the possibility of engaging in the kind of political action which demonstrates the viability of alternatives in practice (*see* Connolly, *Political Science and Ideology*, p. 37).

Initially, social science might well respond by identifying unused resources for action, noting not only who has actually exercised power but also who had the capacity for exercising it—who possesses the available though unused passion, wit, education, and wealth. Beyond this, however, social scientists find it understandably hard to move. How could they recognize underdeveloped resources? In the absence of virtue—or of vice—how can one know of its possible presence?

It is certainly expecting too much of the mass of social scientists to fulfill promises which, as Lionel Trilling has seen, are made by the contemporary novel. Its reader would seem to be better prepared and more demanding than the reader of the literature of social science. The reader of the novel is, after all, more intimately concerned about what has been left undone, about undisplayed experience, about deflected and repressed potentialities. Knowing a good deal of undeveloped resources—knowing the spaces within himself—he is even prepared to assume that there is finally nothing real within and nothing real without. And he turns to the novel not because the novel itself fills the void with finalities, but merely because it evokes previously unexpressed levels of being. "Having come to take nullity for granted," Trilling says, "he wants to be enlightened and entertained by statements about the nature of nothing, what its size is, how it is furnished, what services the management provides, what sort of conversation and amusements can go on in it."[12] The problem is to illuminate the spaces we are capable of clearing, to accept the unobtrusive clue provided by one of the entries in Sei Shōnagon's *Pillow Book:*

---

[12] Lionel Trilling, "James Joyce in His Letters," *Commentary*, 45 (February, 1968), 55.

One bright, moonlit night a messenger thrust a note into the anteroom where I was staying. On a sheet of magnificent scarlet paper I read the words, "There is nothing." It was the moonlight that made this so delightful; I wonder whether I would have enjoyed it at all on a rainy night.

Trilling notes that the theater is especially equipped to reveal the range of nothing and the promise which inheres in some specific nullity:

By means of the irony which it generates merely through turning a conscious eye on its traditional devices of illusion, the theater easily escapes from its servitude to morality into free and radical play with the nature of existence as morality assumes it to be. That life is a dream, that all the world's a stage, that right you are if you think you are—such propositions can be forcibly demonstrated by the theater, which, defined by its function of inducing us to accept appearance as reality, delights in discovering in itself the power of showing that reality is but appearance, in effect nothing.[13]

We may be near to realizing that the modern theater has an affinity to the games which social scientists might play. If part of social science can tell us that existing social systems do indeed exist, another part can playfully, experimentally attempt to create previously unrealized social systems, moving into conceptual vacuums by employing what are literally experimental designs. Such designs reveal environments for action; they clear space we previously thought to be nonexistent. Robert S. Cahill has put the point well: "An epistemological model for the discovery of conditions under which heretofore unrealized states of affairs (but envisioned states of affairs nonetheless) can be realized exists in the form of the experimental design—which, incidentally, constitutes one of the main choreo-

---

[13] *Ibid.*

graphic elements underlying the dance toward truth which science involves."[14]

To create new realities experimentally, the social scientist must first decide how much of possible reality he wishes to bring within his grasp, what, precisely, he will regard as relevant. Failing to stipulate new relevancies, he can only accept whatever happens already to be articulated within his field of operation. His theory of relevance must therefore be derived not merely from what is but also from what exists elsewhere or what might yet be brought into being. That is, his theory must necessarily be idealistic, circumscribing not only what men have done but also what, in his view, they might possibly do.

When social scientists investigate a condition officially defined as a "problem" by the prevailing ideology, they are not impelled to understand the less visible order of phenomena which underlies the officially identified problem. Were they to probe deeper and more radically, to participate in valuation on that more fundamental level where those with power *define* problems, they might perceive dormant patterns and unexpressed commitments. And if they were concerned with articulating such patterns and commitments they might recognize the usefulness of both experiments in simulation and phenomenological approaches.[15]

The social scientist's boundaries, in any case, cannot properly be derived from what is confirmed by the established agencies of private or public government. He must trust his

---

[14] Robert S. Cahill, personal note.

[15] *See* Murray L. Wax, "On Misunderstanding Verstehen: A Reply to Abel," *Sociology and Social Research*, 51 (April, 1967), 323-333, especially p. 328.

own unofficial vision, for it is apt to be more comprehensive than the vision of those who see a problem as urgently in need of solution. And because he is less pressured to respond immediately, because he is less partial, he can be more aware of alternatives. He is more likely to recognize that the solution of an immediately pressing problem will raise additional problems. He can insist on the incompleteness of all offered answers, for his overriding concern is with keeping social systems open, not with getting results. His work implies that the *real* interest of those involved is not necessarily the professed one. To put it bluntly, he knows better—but is saved from arrogance since what he knows is not some specific answer but rather the partiality of all knowledge, the failure implicit in every success.

Consequently the social scientist can accept no definition of a problem as definitive, not even when a virtual consensus on what constitutes the problem may exist. His independence is naturally not easy to maintain: he is likely, in Christian Bay's words, "to agree with the prevailing values of his profession, of the major foundations and of his government, at least on the more basic public policy objectives and assumptions."[16] Whatever the difficulties, he must nevertheless seek to convert sacred realms into secular ones, irrational attitudes (attributed to the masses) into rational beliefs (attributed to self-conscious classes), latent movements into manifest ones. His problem is to include the excluded. For him, exceptions must turn out to prove rules insofar as he can proceed to *make* exceptions into rules.

To create space for exceptions we have finally no alternative other than to act. Only by acting on the basis of our

---

[16] Christian Bay, "Politics and Pseudopolitics," *American Political Science Review*, 59 (March, 1965), 42.

experimental designs can we dispel our stupor and open closed systems. The imperative is to test reality, to make nonevents into events, happenings—things which happen *to* us—into meaningful activities. To do so is to make reality live up to theory or, to put it differently, to give life to theory.

To test social reality—more precisely, to reveal the range of resources for effective action which inhere in an existing social situation—the conventional posture of the participant-observer is insufficient. Merely observing a school, a protest movement, an army unit, a slum neighborhood, or a suburban community as a neutral insider who inoffensively participates in the affairs of the group can yield no more than knowledge of prevailing behavior. Nor do questionnaires eliciting expressions of group desires provide more in understanding. The observer who, in the name of scientific objectivity, fails to *move* his subject cannot reveal that larger truth which includes potentialities in addition to present realities. He cannot learn about repressed or undeveloped capacities. He cannot show that "respondents" who admit to being satisfied employees, prisoners, patients, students, or suburbanites are also somehow troubled or that those who claim to regard themselves as victims and deviants might also regard themselves as autonomous actors. In short, he remains oblivious to potentials for action. If, then, his concern is with disclosing more than manifest reality, he must act as irritant, as *agent provocateur*. Committed to extending the sphere of human action—to creating space for politics, play, public performance—he must *activate* the community. For him, there is finally no other way of getting to *know* society, to know its full promise and its hidden resources. Thus it is in the name of social knowledge—of social science—that he must be activistic.

Were social scientists saints, they might of course simply live exemplary lives within the communities they study, leaving as full a record as they can, *making* a record. Wholly exposed, they would then risk martyrdom, their very vulnerability enraging and finally moving others. They would in any case have induced the community to discover its capacities for action. Yet we might expect social scientists to achieve the same goal by encouraging them to challenge community values directly, by having them inquire—slyly, disingenuously—whether men might not risk more, lead a second life or at least a more various one. "Don't you think," they would have to ask, pretending innocence, "that you could possibly cope with more?" When this kind of question impels men to respond, they will surely strain to change their situation. Thus an existing social order may be enlarged and transformed.

A dramatic illustration of how social science can creatively restructure a prevailing system of power is provided by Robert Rubenstein's and Harold D. Lasswell's *The Sharing of Power in a Psychiatric Hospital*. The authors have called their technique for changing relationships "prototyping" to distinguish it from "experimentation" and "intervention." Experiments, they have said,

> proceed by identifying, measuring, and modifying variables according to plan; the results are amenable to succinct, usually mathematical, summary and precise replication. . . .
>
> Prototyping consists in innovating social practices for the purpose of discovering factors that condition their occurrence and consequences. *A prototype is launched in a context which is only partially controlled by innovators*. . . . The most appro-

priate strategies take the *whole* value-institution context into consideration.

Prototypes are distinguished from "interventions," as well as experiments. An intervention is an innovation which, despite opposition, is officially introduced by the decision-makers of the larger community. If a city is the scene of controversies over the introduction of psychiatrists into the schools, the innovation is part of the arena of power, and concessions must be made to political expediency.[17]

Rubenstein and Lasswell introduced a social innovation into an established system—a mental hospital not wholly dissimilar from other organized communities—so as to put a power structure which had been traditionally exempt from democratic norms to the test. Their innovation consisted of establishing a democratic forum for sharing power. A mental hospital would scarcely seem to be a promising setting for giving the powerless responsibilities by involving them in a process for making key decisions. Yet patients—individuals who had been previously defeated as they struggled for power in their families or in work, school, and professional communities in which they had sought unsuccessfully to participate—began slowly to gain in self-control, literally in self-government. Their participatory activity had the effect of rehabilitating them. It gradually became apparent, furthermore, that if one accepted both psychiatric patients and staff members as participants in the decision-making process, one would have to question the traditional medical-therapeutic model for coping with the behavioral problems of the disadvantaged, persons classified

---

[17] Robert Rubenstein and Harold D. Lasswell, *The Sharing of Power in a Psychiatric Hospital* (New Haven: Yale University Press, 1966), pp. 14-15; emphasis supplied.

as stupefied or irresponsible. One would have to open systems whose closure is generally felt to be reasonable. Admittedly, hierarchies of power within closed systems are frequently accepted as reasonable by virtually everyone, the powerful as well as the powerless, by winners and losers, men and women, whites and blacks, guards and prisoners, teachers and students, nurses and patients. We may all willingly behave as expected, some as superiors and others as subordinates. But the prototype situation created and described by Rubenstein and Lasswell shows that a closed hierarchically organized system is not the most appropriate one for aiding the development of the disadvantaged: role changes and structural innovations are required.

Their work raised an even more radical question concerning the categories which freeze us in our roles. As they put it: "Why physicians? Why nurses? Why the designations 'patient' and 'illness' "?[18] These questions (intoxicating in an otherwise sober book) challenge the most sacred distinctions and can be addressed to many settings. A patient-staff meeting is a social institution which might yet find its parallels in the world outside psychiatric hospitals. Rubenstein and Lasswell rightly see their innovation as a generally attractive model for "transforming the power process for individuals."[19] If hospitals can risk exposure to democratic processes, why not prisons, schools, professional associations, or industrial shops? Why *permanent* establishments of guards, teachers, officials, or managers? Who is healthy and who sick? Who is to say that one category of individuals should have power while another must live without it? Why let anyone have the *last* word?

[18] *Ibid.*, p. 276.
[19] *Ibid.*, p. 14.

I do not wish to be misunderstood: although I am insisting that no one may properly claim the last word, I realize that words remain indispensable to sustain ourselves. Without concepts we would be overwhelmed by a boundless and unstructured continuum, a fearful openness. Concepts enable us to keep our distance from nature, to maintain our conscious selves. They let us *hold* our experience. They establish sequences and patterns. As experience threatens to defeat us, languages serve to *place* it, to make even the most upsetting occurrence all right as we quite literally relate it. Unbalanced by what we see, we are virtually driven to relate our experience to what is conventional. We begin by telling stories, making up things, disguising part of reality, simulating. Seemingly incomprehensible experience is thus put into some perspective—ours. It is contained by metaphors, captured by comparisons. And as it is governed by words, it ceases to be troublesome.

Our languages, establishing relations, give us relief. They help make our experience tolerable by making it intelligible, by assimilating it to the familiar. Using them, we reach the center where others congregate; we enter a conventional community. We have our say for the reason measured out by Donne:

> I thought, if I could draw my paines,
> Through Rimes vexation, I should them allay,
> Griefe brought to numbers cannot be so fierce,
> For he tames it, that fetters it in verse.

Bringing our emotions "to numbers," we make them accessible to others. Communicating with others, we get others to recognize us and our queer feelings. To sustain us, we need recognition. Through our words—or pauses which promise words—we gain the esteem of others, and hence our balance.

But more is involved. The theories which give us security and self-confidence also open unsettling possibilities. They move us into new territories, especially when we have the resources to become venturesome and extravagant. William James has made the point tellingly:

The substitution of concepts and their connections, of a whole conceptual order, in short, for the immediate perceptual flow, thus widens enormously our mental panorama. Had we no concepts we should live simply by "getting" each successive moment of experience, as the sessile sea-anemone on its rock receives whatever nourishment the wash of the waves may bring. With concepts we go in quest of the absent, meet the remote, actively turn this way or that, bend our experience, and make it tell us whither it is bound. We change its order, run it backwards, bring far bits together and separate near bits, jump about over its surface instead of ploughing through its continuity, string its items on as many ideal diagrams as our mind can frame. All these are ways of *handling* the perceptual flux and *meeting* distant parts of it; and as far as this primary function of conception goes, we can only conclude it to be what I began by calling it, a faculty superadded to our barely perceptual consciousness for its use in practically adapting us to a larger environment than that of which brutes take account. We *harness* perceptual reality in concepts in order to drive it better to our ends.[20]

Conceptual systems, provided they map untravelled terrain, can make us move. They can induce those who have arrived at the political center to risk eccentric activities—that is, activities which enlarge the scope of their existence. To do so, our words must intimate how settled and boring things are at the center, and how exciting they might be outside. The test of the success of our words is their capac-

[20] William James, *Some Problems of Philosophy* (New York: Longmans, 1940), p. 51.

ity for engaging us, making us tense by building up suspense. Symbol systems, even in the discipline of political science, must engage us as drama does by making us wonder both where we might come out and how far we might go. Failing to seduce, they leave mindless, antitheoretical forces in society at loose ends. Succeeding, they arouse us, compelling us to participate in the exploration of a reality which might yet acquire meaning for us.

When theory does make us into participants, we are surely obliged to welcome it. However much our experience may be imprisoned within the present armory of abstractions, it is still abstractions which provide that poise and confidence we need to take chances, move ahead, and amplify our existence. At a minimum, our theories give us relief; at best they give us but temporary relief.

Not surprisingly, we remain ambivalent toward them. We esteem them for putting experiences in their place, for putting an end to inquiry. Yet we treat each of our theories with distaste—the distaste we properly have for everything threatening to be definitive. If we must come to conclusions, therefore, as I suppose I must, it becomes imperative not to seem threatening, not to conclude with any specific message on any particular note.

Ideally, we would all write in disappearing ink. We would let the sounds fade out, even while resoundingly affirming that for us as members of a community we have no greater treasure, no finer plaything, than our words and our sounds.

Index

INDEX

The Book Manufacture

Open Systems: Arenas for Political Action was composed, offset printed, and bound by Kingsport Press. The paper is Perkins & Squier Company's Glatfelter Old Forge. Internal and case design was by John Goetz. Ray Lending designed the paperback cover. The book is set in Janson type with Engravers Roman and Janson display type.